ITALY

89-1094

DG417
.I885
1986

ITALY

By the Editors of Time-Life Books
With photographs by Romano Cagnoni

TIME-LIFE BOOKS ∘ ALEXANDRIA, VIRGINIA

$17.50

Cover: Arcaded palaces flank Venice's main thoroughfare, the Grand
Canal, where gondolas lie moored
between their posts.

Pages 1 and 2: The emblem on page 1
includes a star, representing the Italian
nation, superimposed on a cog-
wheel, standing for labor, framed by
branches of oak and olive, which
indicate strength and peace
respectively. Italy's national flag, a
tricolor in green, white and red, is
shown on the following page.

Front and back endpapers: A topo-
graphic map illustrating the major
rivers, mountain ranges and other
natural features of Italy appears on the
front endpaper; the back endpaper
shows the country's 20 regions and
principal towns.

Time-Life Books Inc.
is a wholly owned subsidiary of

TIME INCORPORATED

FOUNDER: Henry R. Luce 1898-1967

Editor-in-Chief: Henry Anatole Grunwald
Chairman and Chief Executive Officer: J. Richard Munro
President and Chief Operating Officer: N. J. Nicholas Jr.
Chairman of the Executive Committee: Ralph P. Davidson
Corporate Editor: Ray Cave
Executive Vice President, Books: Kelso F. Sutton
Vice President, Books: George Artandi

TIME-LIFE BOOKS INC.

EUROPEAN EDITOR: Kit van Tulleken
Assistant European Editor: Gillian Moore
Design Director: Ed Skyner
Photography Director: Pamela Marke
Chief of Research: Vanessa Kramer
Chief Sub-editor: Ilse Gray

LIBRARY OF NATIONS

Series Editor: Tony Allan

Editorial Staff for *Italy*
Editor: Gillian Moore
Researcher: Lesley Coleman
Designer: Lynne Brown
Sub-editor: Sally Rowland
Picture Department: Christine Hinze, Peggy Tout
Editorial Assistant: Molly Oates

EDITORIAL PRODUCTION

Chief: Jane Hawker
Production Assistants: Alan Godwin, Maureen Kelly
Editorial Department: Theresa John, Debra Lelliott,
Sylvia Osborne

Valuable help was given in the preparation of this
volume by Bona Schmid and Anna Polo (Milan), and
Ann Natanson (Rome).

Contributors: The chapter texts were written by
Iain Carson, Frederic V. Grunfeld, Robert Harvey
and Alan Lothian.

Assistant Editor for the U.S. Edition:
Barbara Fairchild Quarmby

CONSULTANTS

Dr. Denis Mack Smith is Senior Research
Fellow of All Souls College, Oxford,
England. He has written many books on
modern Italian history.

John Haycraft, Director General of
International House, a group of English-
language schools, has recently completed a
book on Italy entitled *Italian Labyrinth*.

PHOTOGRAPHER

Romano Cagnoni was born in Tuscany, but
he has lived in London since 1958.
Journalistic assignments have taken him to
most of the world's trouble spots, including
Biafra, Vietnam, Afghanistan and the
Middle East. He has also photographed
many aspects of his native Italy. He
traveled in Italy for three months to shoot
the photographs for this volume in the
Library of Nations series.

Library of Congress Cataloguing in Publication Data
Italy.
    (Library of nations)
    Bibliography: p.
    Includes index.
    1. Italy. I. Cagnoni, Romano. II. Time-Life Books.
III. Series: Library of nations (Alexandria, Va.)
DG417.I885 1986   945.092   86-14456
ISBN 0-8094-5156-5
ISBN 0-8094-5311-8 (lib. bdg.)

CONTENTS

Pale November sunlight filters through a grove of Tuscan olive trees onto nets spread out to catch the ripe fruit when the branches are shaken. The olive

has for centuries been an agricultural staple in Italy, which vies with Spain to produce the world's largest annual olive-oil yield.

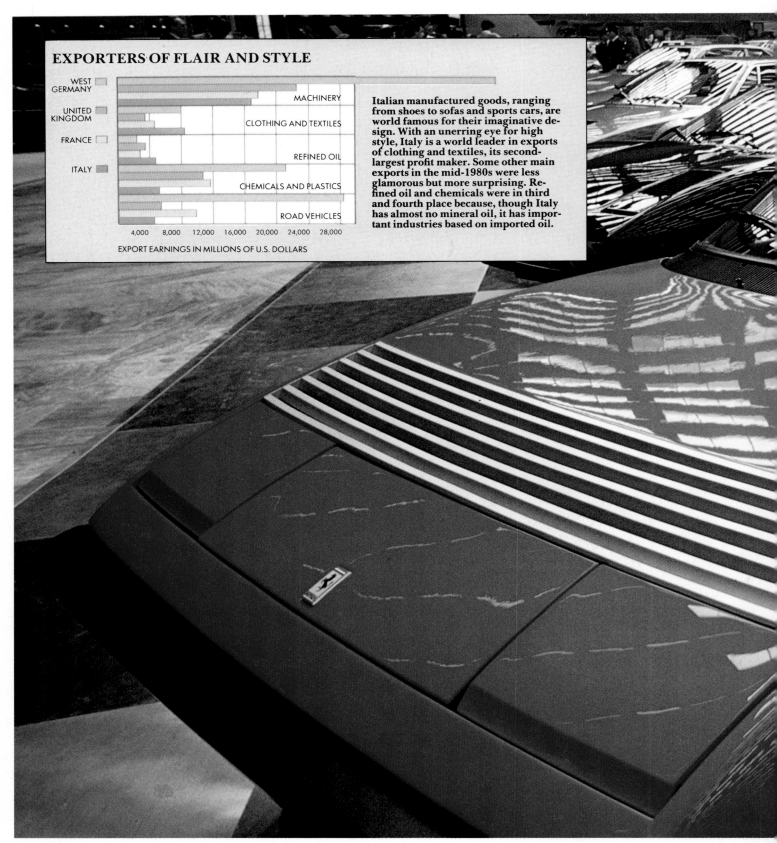

EXPORTERS OF FLAIR AND STYLE

WEST GERMANY	MACHINERY
UNITED KINGDOM	CLOTHING AND TEXTILES
FRANCE	REFINED OIL
ITALY	CHEMICALS AND PLASTICS
	ROAD VEHICLES

4,000   8,000   12,000   16,000   20,000   24,000   28,000

EXPORT EARNINGS IN MILLIONS OF U.S. DOLLARS

Italian manufactured goods, ranging from shoes to sofas and sports cars, are world famous for their imaginative design. With an unerring eye for high style, Italy is a world leader in exports of clothing and textiles, its second-largest profit maker. Some other main exports in the mid-1980s were less glamorous but more surprising. Refined oil and chemicals were in third and fourth place because, though Italy has almost no mineral oil, it has important industries based on imported oil.

A Ferrari painted gleaming scarlet — the traditional Italian color at international motor races — reflects the overhead lights at the biennial Turin car show.

Sports-car manufacturers such as Maserati, Lamborghini and Ferrari produce only a few thousand vehicles a year, and 80 percent of them are exported.

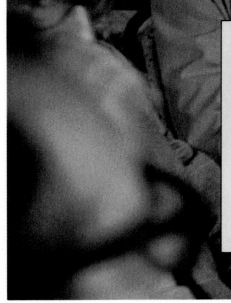

THE NORTHWARD MIGRATION

In the years since World War II, Italy has experienced a remarkable internal migration that is radically altering its demographic make-up. Drawn by the prospect of regular employment in the factories of Milan, Turin and the surrounding small towns, the work force of the rural south is shifting north. In Piedmont and Lombardy, the population grew by 3.5 million between 1951 and 1981. Prosperous Turin, home of the giant Fiat auto factory, has seen its postwar population double. Meanwhile, the populations of six rural regions in the south and center are shrinking, while several others are barely holding their own.

Peasants from the impoverished south of Italy have long been willing to pull up stakes. Until the postwar years, however, their destinations were other European countries or the opposite side of the Atlantic, and they traveled in both directions: 29 million emigrated and 20 million returned between 1861 and 1975. The northward tide of one million migrants annually is now creating less reverse migration. Yet the southerners are not integrated into their new environment. They live apart from the native northerners and cling fiercely to their own traditions.

Scrutinized by a cluster of companions, southern-bred workers play cards in a garden in Valletta, a migrants' suburb outside Turin. Lodged in characterless

apartment complexes, the migrants keep alive some aspects of clannish Mediterranean social life.

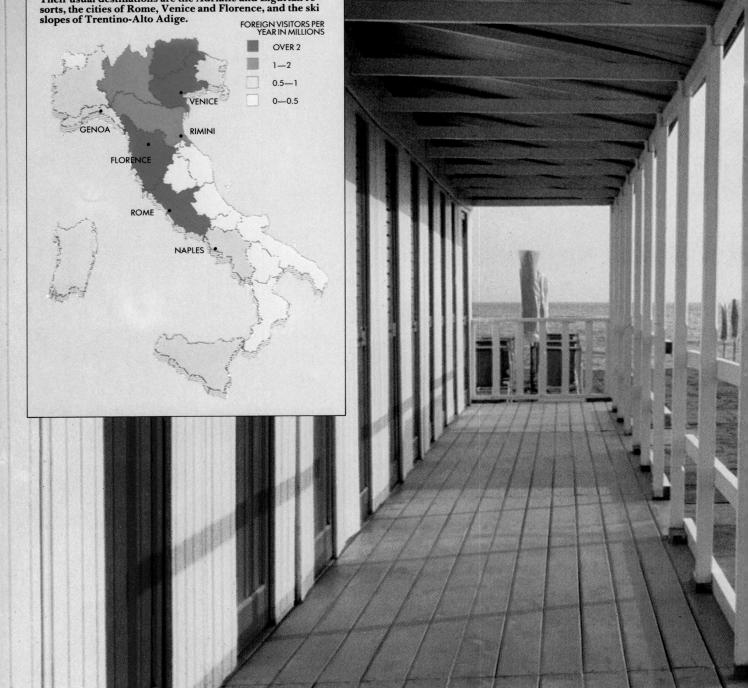

AN ATTRACTION FOR TOURISTS

With about 20 million visitors a year, Italy earns more — 10 billion dollars annually — from tourism than any other European country. In the mid-1980s, vacationers from the United States made up 14 percent of the tourist population, Germans 30 percent, and other Europeans 45 percent. Their usual destinations are the Adriatic and Ligurian resorts, the cities of Rome, Venice and Florence, and the ski slopes of Trentino-Alto Adige.

FOREIGN VISITORS PER
YEAR IN MILLIONS

OVER 2
1—2
0.5—1
0—0.5

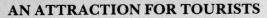

Evening sun bathes a deserted beach at Forte dei Marmi on the Tuscan coast. At the end of the afternoon, when the vacationers decamp, beach attendants

clear the litter, rake the sand and straighten the deck chairs in readiness for the next day's onslaught.

A PASSION FOR SPORTS

The Italians adore soccer with a passion that is matched in few other countries. More than a quarter of a million spectators watch first-division matches live, and many thousands more devotedly attend the games of the other three divisions and the countless clashes between amateur teams. No fewer than three national daily papers are dedicated exclusively to sports — chiefly soccer — and on Mondays, after the big matches, serious newspapers devote half their pages to the game. Soccer players are among the highest-paid employees in the country, and Italian teams have attracted a high proportion of the world's best players.

One reason for the excitement generated by the game is the strength of regional loyalties. Italy became a unified nation fairly recently — in 1861 — and ancient rivalries between the city-states that made up the peninsula have never been forgotten. They are revived by every confrontation in the stadiums — whether between neighboring towns' teams or between giants such as Roma and Turin's Juventus.

Lines of red shirts belonging to members of a local soccer club hang out to dry in a garden in Cortona, Tuscany. Because of a shortage of grassy fields,

Italian amateur players often practice on asphalt — a surface that demands deft ball control and quick maneuvers, hallmarks of the national style.

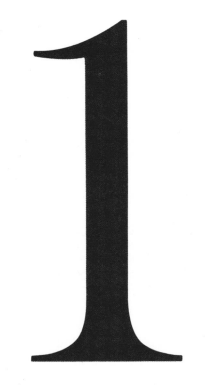

1

Before sitting down to a festive lunch, a proud Sicilian family smiles for a photograph to commemorate a young girl's first Holy Communion. About 60 percent of Italian children take this step — usually at the age of eight — although less than one third of the population now attends church regularly.

THE STRENGTH OF THE FAMILY

"Povera Italia," the Italians like to say, especially after a good meal with good friends. The food has been, as always, excellent, the wine simple and delicious. So it ought to be, the guests are assured: It was made in the cellar of the host's brother-in-law's uncle. A little *grappa* — a spirit distilled from grape stalks and skins — may be offered with the coffee. It too is wholesome and genuine, as indeed it was bound to be, since the man who distilled it is the host's wife's second cousin.

"Poor Italy," the guests agree, as they settle down to an enthusiastic conversation on the trials and tribulations of Italian daily life. The current scandal afflicting the government is certainly a topic; so are the near-impossibility of speedy or intelligent service from the state-owned power or telephone company, the flagrant way a local politician is handing out contracts to relatives and supporters, the incredible delays in postal services. Perhaps another *grappa?* The guests decline. They have a long way to drive home along the *autostrada;* and conversation turns for a moment to a comparison between the latest Alfa Romeo and the newest Lancia. To some of the guests, neither of the cars is out of reach.

Not so long ago, Italy — or large portions of it, anyway — was genuinely poor. As late as 1951 it was predominantly an agricultural country, with more than 40 percent of the labor force working on the land. It was prosperous, for the most part, in the north; almost wealthy, even, around the few industrial cities. But the south was trapped in deep poverty and nowhere, north or south, did Italy's standard of living seriously compare with that of its Western European neighbors. In 1953, a Parliamentary commission on poverty reported that 24 percent of households were either "destitute" or "in hardship"; that 52 percent of homes in the south were without running drinking water and only 57 percent had a lavatory. Rocketing growth rates in the 1950s and 1960s (exceeded only by Japan's) changed all that, and Italy is now a thriving industrial state.

Measured by almost every index of well-being, the Italians are better off than most of them imagined possible. They eat better; they have better education; fewer of their babies die and most adults live longer. In the crasser terms of consumer goods — telephones, cars, washing machines and television sets — Italian ownership approaches, matches and sometimes even exceeds the Western European average. True, the well-being is not evenly distributed: Discrepancies between rich and poor are high by European standards; and the south still lags well behind the north, but even there things have improved beyond all recognition.

The Italians have not only achieved the most astounding economic transformation in Western Europe; they have managed something perhaps

17

1

more difficult. They have retained a great many of the civilized habits of everyday life that have long attracted outsiders to their land. They care about good food and good wine not only for their own sakes, but for the fellowship and conversation that go with them. They like to talk: Italian bars, for instance, are noted more for animated discussion than for serious drinking; and on market day in a small community the cumulative murmur of townsfolk simply chattering — rarely shouting — can be deafening.

Every day the social network is reinforced by the great Italian institution of the *passeggiata,* a kind of mass stroll that takes place in most small towns and many large ones in the early evening. It is at once a fashion parade for the young and a little light exercise for the elderly, a chance for townwide gossip, an unstructured appointment system and an opportunity to renew acquaintances. With a wave, a handshake, a friendly clasp on the shoulder, neighbors can be seen dispensing affection and goodwill. An outsider in an Italian community almost inevitably comes away with an impression of a stable, vigorous and close-knit society.

Yet with so much to be glad about, Italians persist in lamenting their country's failings. An opinion survey carried out in the mid-1980s throughout the European Community revealed that only 6 percent of Italians counted themselves "very happy"; no other country except Greece scored so low. Most Italians would describe themselves as fatalists rather than pessimists; they may, indeed, be the most contented people in the world, though superstitiously convinced that to admit it would bring bad luck. But their woes are real enough; life can be difficult indeed in one of the richest industrial countries in the world.

To begin with, there is the chronic weakness of Italian governments, which makes the economic miracle of the postwar decades seem more than usually miraculous. An achievement of such magnitude is more easily understood where there is a stable and efficient, even authoritarian, state working in harmonious consensus with an ener-

getic, disciplined people; Germany is an obvious example. Yet the Italian economic feat is even more remarkable than Germany's postwar recovery. The two countries' economies grew at about the same rate in the 1950s; but in the 1960s, when Germany's growth slowed down a little, Italy's accelerated, reaching an annual average of more than 6 percent during the whole second half of the decade. In order to achieve this remarkable result, the Italians have had to make do with little more than their own astonishing dynamism.

Since its founding in 1946, the Italian republic has had more than 40 governments, some lasting less than a month. Such transience in the corridors of power is by no means the symptom of instability that it at first appears, since every government has been a coalition dominated by the Christian Democrat Party, and each government has contained most of the same ministers — perhaps in different ministries — as its predecessor; but most coalitions have spent more time locked in internal wrangling than they have spent governing the country. Laws both minor and major have inevitably been compromises, sometimes so badly drafted that they are almost impossible to implement — if, that is, a reliable way of implementing them even existed.

The administration of the Italian state is, indeed, a byword for delay, complexity and sheer incompetence. A country can easily live with rapidly changing governments if it is equipped with a good civil service: France in the 1950s, for example, was characterized by governmental chaos worse than Italy's. But the icily efficient and superbly trained French administrative system saw to it that the nation nevertheless carried on with its postwar reconstruc-

tion. In Italy, though, the administration is out of control. The government spends more than 50 percent of the gross national product, and many experts agree that it misuses a large proportion of that colossal sum.

A 1984 report on the near-paralysis of the Italian civil service by the Formez Research Institute needed 14,000 pages to do justice to its subject. Its painstaking authors found terrifying examples of waste and delay. Take the small farmer whose crops had been ruined by hail. He sought one of the emergency loans offered by a benevolent government, and he got it — three years later, after his application had been processed by no fewer than 10 different offices. Or consider the war widow who spent decades standing in lines and enduring bureaucratic rebuffs before she obtained her meager pension. Most Italians, who have to deal with the system with distressing frequency in

the course of their lives, could recount similar stories.

The investigators discovered a backlog of 450,000 outstanding files in Rome's Treasury Ministry alone, and everywhere a bloated work force that arrived late and left early — usually to go on to a second job. There is no sign that things are likely to get much better; indeed, since Italy's bureaucrats have been buying job-lots of computers with scarcely any attempt to fit them into a logical work system, there is every likelihood that things will get much worse.

The judicial system is in even graver condition. Occasionally outright chicanery weakens faith in its integrity; more damaging still, its desperate slowness destroys faith in its utility. In the recent past, prisoners sometimes spent many years in jail awaiting trial; new laws in the mid-1980s have limited preventive detention, with the result that some potential criminals must be released be-

In the isolated highlands of Abruzzi, men and women share the arduous work of gathering straw after threshing wheat. Most farmers are nearly self-sufficient for food; they grow vegetables and grapes, raise chickens and shoot game for the pot.

fore coming to trial. Civil suits in the 1970s could expect a waiting time of 10 years, and despite attempts to streamline procedures, delays of three or four years were common a decade later.

The educational system also has major defects. Schooling is compulsory only for children aged six to 14, but most children stay on longer in the hope — often disappointed — of getting a better job, or any job at all. And while expenditures on education have risen steadily over the years, almost all the money has been spent on staff. Thus, though Italy has the most favorable teacher-pupil ratio in the European Community, many schools are overcrowded and woefully underequipped.

In the south, where the problem is most acute, many schools operate a two-shift system, in the mornings and afternoons. Almost everywhere, instruction is uninspired and routine. Science teaching is often rudimentary, and children are ill-prepared to enter a rapidly changing high-technology society. "The curriculum goes back at least 40 years," said one disillusioned teacher in Naples. "Old-fashioned rote learning: It's completely out of touch with what the kids need. What's more, the kids know it." She added, bitterly, "For them, school has become no more than a parking place between childhood and unemployment."

Universities are grossly overcrowded as well, because there is no ceiling imposed on student numbers. They produce hordes of arts graduates at the expense of much-needed scientists and engineers. Such an ill-balanced output is one of the reasons for Italy's high teacher-pupil ratio, but even an overstaffed education system and a swollen public service between them are unable to absorb the flood of degree-waving

In towns the length of Italy, balconies serve as forums for gossip and as observation posts from which to scan the bustle of neighborhood life. They also provide cramped apartment dwellers with a welcome modicum of extra space for plants and laundry.

hopefuls. Italy suffers from a steadily worsening problem of graduate unemployment. The authorities worry about the political discontent that it generates, but they have not taken action.

The universities also produce more medical practitioners than most other countries. Italy's national health service is terribly costly, and throughout the country, the salaries of medical personnel and administrators swallow up far too large a proportion of the funds available. In parts of the south, hospital patients often have to rely on relatives for food and clean bedding. In Milan, at the hub of Italian prosperity, it is not unheard of for major hospitals to close their doors to emergency admissions while the staff is struggling with a backlog of patients lying on cots crammed into dirty corridors.

Other welfare services are no more enviable. Until the mid-1970s, social security was practically nonexistent. Unemployment pay is still pitifully low and, although old-age pensions have vastly increased, actually obtaining one can involve a citizen in a prolonged and exhausting struggle with a notoriously unhelpful officialdom.

And over the whole Italian state hangs the unedifying aroma of corruption. A selection of newspaper stories that were published during one summer month in the mid-1980s is representative of what goes on all the time. One sequence of articles concerned a crisis in the government: A minister had been accused of belonging to a secret Masonic society whose least sinister purpose appeared to be the enrichment of its members. Then there was a report from Spain: Italian magistrates were struggling to extradite a former general of Italy's Financial Police, who was wanted for his part in a revenue

1

fraud worth billions of lira. Simultaneously, correspondents on the island of Sicily sent news of a government inspector whose duty was to ensure that wine and food were not adulterated by sharp operators — who had himself been arrested for adulteration.

These were only the few who were caught. The newspapers also presented a sober report on outrageous under-declarations of income to the tax authorities by small businesses and members of the professions: the fashionable Roman ice-cream parlors that reported serving only 40 patrons a day; the successful lawyers who mysteriously earned less than a third of their office rentals. The government was engaged in trying to stamp out tax fraud, but such stories show how monumental a task it had set itself. And as a crowning irony, the newspapers announced that the Pope had just awarded a prize to a theologian who declared that hell indeed existed, but might well be empty. It came as no surprise to cynical Italians; even in the next world, they knew, the rascals would go scot-free.

Anywhere else, such a background of institutional chaos and corruption would signify not the brink of disaster but disaster itself, a country plunging into ruin and misery. Yet Italians are not merely surviving but flourishing. Observers find themselves asking two questions. The first is obvious: How do they manage so well? The second follows when the stranger has realized that Italians are not the crazy, easygoing romantics of legend, but a tough, shrewd and hard-headed people. Then comes the question: Why on earth do they put up with such a situation?

Both questions share a single answer, and it lies in one institution in which Italians do place their faith. It is an institution with no headquarters building and no supporting bureaucracy. It protects Italians from misgovernment even as it ensures that misgovernment is inevitable. That institution is the family. Its members sustain one another not only with supplies of homemade wine and *grappa,* but with assiduous maneuvering to protect one another's interests in the outside world.

The key position of the family in Italian life is largely the result of the nation's turbulent history. Nominally united under the Romans, by the fourth century A.D. the Italian peninsula was fragmented, and for the next 13 centuries large parts of it fell under foreign rule. Arbitrary and corrupt government by unsympathetic strangers was the lot of most Italians, and wars were all too frequent. The unification of Italy in 1861 did very little to increase ordinary Italians' involvement with their state. The vote was denied to illiterates — who made up two-thirds of the population.

To the poverty-stricken southerners, especially, Parliament seemed remote and irrelevant, and in the course of the 1860s the south was torn by guerrilla warfare and bloody uprisings. In the 20th century, under Mussolini, Italy experienced strong centralized government for the first time since the Roman Empire — but the excesses of fascism traumatized the nation even more than centuries of misrule by foreigners.

With so little experience of wise and just government, Italians have turned to smaller, domestic units for everyday succor and support. To an Italian, the family is a fortress, a defended position within which the virtues of loyalty, honesty, discipline, foresight and self-sacrifice — all sadly lacking in Italy's public life — are exercised almost automatically. The family is also a vehicle for progress — its own progress.

And therein lies the rub. What benefits one family does not necessarily benefit all the others: The idea of the general good has never taken deep root in Italy. Authority is rarely respected in its own, abstract right. The agencies of the state, far from representing impersonal pillars of national administration, are merely examples of someone else's family getting ahead. Those in positions of power, the winning players in the great game, have to be treated with respect, placated if necessary and deceived if possible by other, lesser players who are seeking advantage for their own families.

Hence the apparent shamelessness of much of Italian public life, and the relative tolerance extended to corrupt officials. In many Italians, outrage is blended with a sneaking admiration. On a much smaller scale, indeed, most of them play the same game. Any self-respecting family can lay claim to some sort of network of contacts, without which the simplest transactions — especially those involving the state bureaucracy — can be both exhausting and time-consuming. One southerner, busily engaged in trading favors to acquire the recommendation from a local politician that would ensure his son a job, explained the Catch-22 reasoning that has kept the system alive so long. "Of course it would be better for everybody if nobody did this sort of thing," he said. "But everybody who can, does — so what do you expect from me? Listen, my boy needs that job."

But if the system generates public anarchy, it also creates a good deal of private stability. Family life, after all, is the bedrock of human society; and habits

Completely absorbed in each other's company, mothers and sons of two generations stroll beside the Grand Canal in Venice. The powerful bond between a young boy and his mother does not diminish even when the son stands a head taller than *mamma*.

of decency at home provide at least some moderating influence on public excesses. Take, for example, the hosts who were enjoying a *grappa* with their guests. The older members of that household will remember the extended family life that prevailed in Italy until a generation ago. They may romanticize the past a little, recalling how children, parents and grandparents all lived together, sharing a joint livelihood, meeting two or three times a day for meals that were really social sacraments presided over by a twinkling-eyed patriarch with a notoriously soft spot for the young. They will not, however, forget the squalor of overcrowding and the sheer brutal labor that was the lot of the great majority.

In today's easier circumstances, Italy is becoming a nation of nuclear families: Fewer than 10 percent of households have more than five members. But most Italian adults still live near their parents and visit them regularly. Their sense of family solidarity, of shared goals, of respect for elders and love for children will be as strong as anything their parents felt.

Italians take children seriously, and they take boy children especially seriously, because the family is male-oriented — although not, perhaps, as male-dominated as most outsiders and many Italian men imagine it to be, or as it once was. Certainly, the boy child is treated as a little king — spoiled, flattered, encouraged to be articulate and continually assured of his own charm. He will grow up, with any luck, into a self-confident, sensitive young man; his sensitivity, though somewhat likely to include an excessive fear of ridicule, of making a fool of himself, will allow him to have a closer and easier relationship with women than men of

northern nations can usually manage. This is one of his mother's gifts to him — one of many, for in Italy a son is his mother's masterpiece.

The bond between Italian men and their mothers is probably, for good or ill, the most powerful social tie in the country, and it has led to the somewhat startling phenomenon of *mammismo*. The word is impossible to translate and the concept behind it difficult to elucidate. It describes both the lifelong need of a man for the kind of maternal attention he was given in childhood, as well as the even greater need felt by many mothers to continue to provide it. It accounts for the immense influence Italian women have usually been able to wield in an ostensibly patriarchal society, where their legal rights until recently were very much less extensive than those of men.

Indeed, if an Italian boy is raised as a king, a little girl is trained from birth to be the quiet power behind the throne. She is taught to be self-effacing, less extroverted than her brother, even secretive. Her role is to be that of wife and eventually mother, bringing up her own sons in turn as the family's greatest glory while she passes on to her daughters the legacy of quiet cleverness and moral strength that actually holds the family together.

The harder the family situation, the tougher the Italian women become; and the more obvious the apparent patriarchy, the more developed the feminine sinews underneath. In rural southern Italy, for example, women are ostensibly little more than appendages of their husbands and fathers, and often they are beasts of burden as well. Yet acute observers have noted that it is the women who make the real decisions in most communities, who

keep them functioning in conditions of grinding poverty that send the men helplessly to the wineshops, where they grumble in despair.

In gentler circumstances, when they can afford to look beyond mere survival, Italian women set much store by family meals. Italians spend a higher proportion of their incomes on food than do the people of other industrialized nations. Every housewife who can will shop frequently, putting a premium on freshness; the food she prepares will be simple, plentiful and excellent. Respect for meals was long reflected in working hours throughout most of Italy, especially in the hotter climate of the south: Shops and offices closed for anything up to four hours in the middle of the day, allowing everybody time for a long nap after a substantial lunch. This pattern is weakening, however, as society changes.

Sons and daughters who have left home come back for regular family gatherings and, since most dwellings are too small for entertaining on a large scale, restaurants do a good business. Nephews, nieces, uncles, aunts and cousins of various generations may well appear around the table: A good family party is a big family party.

Through institutions such as the extended family gathering and the evening stroll, Italy's millions of family "nation-states" ensure that they do not exist in isolation. Like real nation-states, each family binds itself to others by webs of alliance spun from mutual interest. Although each is willing to stretch and twist the fabric of Italian society to achieve its own ends, it is in the interests of none to destroy the fabric altogether.

Had any wished to do so, it would have found a formidable opponent in

the self-proclaimed defender of the family, the Roman Catholic Church. The role of the church in Italian political and social history has been profound. To Italians, the papacy is almost a national institution. Apart from seven turbulent decades in the 14th century, when the popes resided in Avignon, the head of the Catholic Church has always been based in Rome. And until 1870, part of the country was under direct papal rule. Throughout the peninsula, the church provided the only social services Italians knew; even today, it supplements the state-provided health and welfare services. Religious orders run some of the best schools in the country, which are patronized by the affluent élite. In the rural communities of the

past, the parish priest was the natural leader, the man to whom families turned with problems and questions of all kinds. Even today, the church's moral authority is tremendous.

Italian society has needed all the strength at its disposal to withstand the buffetings of the last few decades. The transformation of a deeply traditional, agrarian people into a thriving, dynamic industrial state compressed into three short decades a social evolution that elsewhere in Europe took at least a century. The Big Bang, one writer called it with pardonable hyperbole, and Italians can still hear the ringing in their ears.

For millions of families, economic

growth has meant a traumatic move from the countryside to the cities — above all, from the countryside of the south to the cities of the north. Since 1951, about 10 million people (six million according to notoriously unreliable government statistics, and at least double that figure according to some informed observers) have uprooted themselves from the land and settled in Turin, Milan and the other industrial centers. The traditions of family life were a product of the old, agricultural Italy, an Italy of poverty and hardship, small towns and stubborn peasant farmers. The migrants to the cities have been hard put to retain them.

In the early days of the great industrialization, rural men often set off

EATING WELL ALLA ITALIANA

A market stall is piled high with dried beans.

Salami and sausages in all shapes and sizes hang in a Tuscan shop.

A modern ice-cream parlor displays its range of flavors.

Chili peppers glow beside olives picked at every stage of ripeness.

Shoppers contemplate festooned ranks of Italian cheeses.

A *pasticceria* offers a selection of cakes, pastries and sweets.

Good food is one of life's great pleasures for the Italians, who show their appreciation in the clearest way. They spend a larger proportion of their incomes on food than any other Western European people.

It is not that they have lavish tastes; pasta, the closest thing to a national dish, is one of the most economical of foods. Pasta and rice rarely fail to appear in one form or another in a typical family meal. Pasta or rice will usually be followed by meat or fish, vegetables — which the Italians eat in greater quantities than any other people in Europe — a salad, and fruit or cheese. Elaborate desserts seldom appear on the family table, although it is customary for guests to bring a cake bought from one of the excellent pastry shops to be found throughout the country.

What distinguishes such a meal is the quality and freshness of its ingredients. Good cooking starts in the markets, which most Italian cooks visit daily. Frozen and canned foods have little place in the kitchen, and the supermarket has yet to replace the family stall or small shop offering farm-fresh fruit and vegetables. As a result, Italy has Europe's highest number of retail food outlets — more than four times as many as West Germany, for example.

The markets also display in profusion the preserved foods — ham, sausage, cheese and dried beans — that even in the recent past were an essential means of storing summer's plenty against winter's dearth. Many preserved foods are prepared by time-consuming methods and are priced accordingly: Parmesan cheese, for example, is aged two to four years, and the most mature is considered the choicest. For Italians, using less-expensive substitutes would be an affront to tradition and their own discriminating tastes.

alone to seek factory jobs. They lived in barracks-like conditions in northern cities, sending most of their new wages to their families — women and children — in the villages back home. Normal family living was impossible, but men and women alike at least had the consolation that the sacrifices were for the good of the family and that, however agonizing the experience, they were making progress.

By the late 1960s, however, with waves of immigrants still flooding into the jerry-built slums that had been erected around the periphery of the northern cities, the novelty of regular earnings had worn off, and with it a good deal of the initial optimism. Wages were not high; job security was minimal, state welfare benefits practically nonexistent; unemployment, especially among the young, was a growing problem. Moreover, the old supportive networks of extended family relationships had been shriveled by their translation to ill-planned, overcrowded cities. The sharply differentiated roles of men and women, which had seemed inevitable in a rural community, made much less sense in industrial cities; changes in the roles of the sexes were affecting family values. The younger generation had neither memories of the old ways to sustain it nor a secure place in the new industrial society to compensate. Strains within families multiplied, and losses began to outweigh gains.

There arose a twofold dissatisfaction with the brash consumer society that had come into existence in little more than a decade's time. On the one hand, a great many ordinary people saw themselves being excluded from a fair share in the well-being they were creating. On the other hand, a new genera-

tion of the educated young rejected the consumer society entirely and demanded nothing less than a revolution.

The spectacle of student revolt was by no means confined to Italy, of course. In most Western countries, 1968 was a heady year for privileged youth. But in Italy, the *sessantottini* — the "sixty-eighters," as a whole generation of more-or-less radicalized young intellectuals would be called — came of age in a society already in turmoil as a result of the rapid social changes it was living through. Some of the sixty-eighters were prepared to go a good deal further than their fellow radicals in other countries.

The means by which the extremists sought to topple what they regarded as a hopelessly corrupt state were assassinations, bombings and kidnappings. They began in 1968 and reached a peak 10 years later, in 1978, with the kidnapping and murder of former Prime Minister Aldo Moro by terrorists belonging to the Marxist Red Brigades. The Italian police at first seemed powerless to deal with the menace.

But the murder of Moro — not to mention close to 2,500 other terrorist attacks that year — galvanized the Italian authorities into action. Just as important, it sickened the public. Efficient police work and a new public commitment to cooperation with the authorities crippled the terrorists, who began to fight among themselves. The fabric of society turned out to be stronger than the terrorists had imagined.

One of the reasons for its strength was that other campaigns succeeded in transforming society by peaceful means. The 1970s saw a vast rise in the real incomes of most ordinary Italians as well as the enactment of legislation for employment security and at last the

creation of a welfare state of sorts. It was a stormy decade, by any standards, and it inspired plenty of gloom-laden writing from commentators both inside and outside the country. Yet Italy was clearly in better shape at the end of it than at its beginning.

Women, for example, were no longer obviously second-class citizens. More of them were now going out to work. Peasant women always had, of course; but, in the north especially, women were taking jobs at all levels in the Italian economy, in a pattern that closely reflected the other Western European countries. A quarter of Italian doctors now are women, for example — a figure that would have been unthinkable in the immediate postwar years.

Legislation passed in the late 1960s and the 1970s was at last giving them rights that at least partly matched those of their husbands. A law allowing an adulterous wife to be imprisoned was repealed, for instance; married women were officially given the right to a half share in a couple's property. (Five-month maternity leaves at full pay had been granted years before.) It will take time for these changes in the law to gradually work their way through to everyday family life. But even in the south, where traditions die hardest, it is clear that the old male-dominated ways cannot last forever.

Perhaps the most startling developments of all, in a country where 97 percent of the population are baptized Catholics, were the legalization of divorce in 1970 and of abortion in 1978 — despite the implacable opposition of the church. Such reforms were partly the result of declining ecclesiastical influence; only around 30 percent of the population attends church regularly, compared with nearly 60 percent in the 1950s. Perhaps, too, they were possible because Italians long ago learned not to take tirades from the pulpit too seriously: They have lived with the church for centuries, after all, and although they will listen respectfully to what their parish priest has to say to them, they are prepared on occasion to choose their own way afterward.

The delay in legalizing divorce stemmed from the fact that the interests of the church and those of Italian families coincided: Italian women, especially, suspected that divorce would simply allow their husbands to throw them out with no financial support. Yet the dire prediction made by the Catholic Church—that divorce would be the death of the Italian family—has not been borne out by experience. After an initial surge, the divorce rate in Italy had settled down by the early 1980s to 13,000 a year—0.2 per 1,000 inhabitants, compared with 2.8 per 1,000 in Britain and 1.7 per 1,000 in Catholic France.

Abortion, despite the teachings of the Catholic Church, existed in Italy long before it was legalized. As in many other countries, Italian women have always practiced abortion—legal or not—along with whatever other methods of birth control were available. The rate of abortion is now the highest in Europe after Denmark. But Italians have never seen abortion or contraception as threats to family life. Instead, they are thought to strengthen it, by reducing illegitimate births and encouraging small families in which each child can be sure of the loving attention that Italians like to give their offspring.

Although the new laws may not be responsible for undermining the social order, there is evidence of something seriously amiss in the Italian family, and it comes in the form of drugs. Since the mid-1970s, the strains of rapid social change have been augmented by the same alarming youth unemployment that afflicts most of the world's developed nations. When even the most assiduously cultivated family connections are insufficient to find a job, many youngsters seek escape through drugs.

Though the problem may be under-standable, its extent is worrisome. As in several other countries, heroin addicts in Italy are supposed to register with the authorities, and in the early 1980s the country had 20,000, compared with 30,000 in West Germany and 10,000 in Great Britain. But the registered addicts are only a fraction of the total, and in Italy they seem to be a smaller fraction than elsewhere. Surveys and hearsay, admittedly unreliable, suggest that the situation in Italy is more serious than in other parts of Europe—and worsening after the fall in heroin prices of the mid-1980s.

Drug addiction is not restricted to any one region or social class. It is as much a menace in southern cities, where traditional attitudes supposedly still prevail, as it is in the big northern metropolises with their uprooted, immigrant populations. University students and the unemployed in the slums are almost equally at risk; the only common factor seems to be the youth of the victims, for practically all are under 30. And drug-taking on this scale is not only a symptom of social stress: It is also a prime cause of it. At the very least, it breeds lawlessness, as addicts turn to crime in order to feed their expensive habit. By the early 1980s, 30 percent of Italy's prison population—itself a high figure by European standards, at 43,000—were addicts.

One of the most alarming aspects of the problem is the speed with which it has developed in Italy. Explains Nicola Dellisanti, one of the organizers of a nationwide drug rehabilitation plan, "Up until 1972 or 1973, drug-taking here was insignificant. We were a conduit in the international drug trade, perhaps. But never a market." So why the explosion? "I'd say 50 percent because of the crisis young Italians are go-ing through: a crisis of traditional values, a crisis in the family generally, little crises in lots of families. Despair." And the other 50 percent? "Because suddenly the drugs were there." And so, Dellisanti might have added, was the money to buy them.

It is a bitter irony that the source of all these family-wrecking narcotics is itself a family business—the world's most sinister. The Mafia, in fact, represents the idea of family loyalty taken to a murderous extreme. It is in many ways a dark mirror in which the image of Italian society at large is reflected, horribly distorted but not unrecognizable; and since society has been busily transforming itself, so has the Mafia.

Like the rest of Italian society, the Mafia has deep, traditional roots. It began in western Sicily, which is still its heartland, and at first it was more a manner of behavior than anything as structured as a secret criminal organization. Law and order in that turbulent and roadless province were almost nonexistent: In order to avoid being swallowed up in the general turmoil, a man had to be ready to avenge any slight, real or imagined, to his own honor or that of his family.

The six orbs on the arms of the Medici, the great Renaissance banking family, are said to represent the weights with which moneychangers checked coins. A 16th-century king of France honored the Medici by letting them use three *fleurs-de-lis* from his own arms.

1

To make oneself respected in the community — that was what counted. The more violence a man was prepared to use, the more respect he enjoyed, and murder became a high road to social advancement. In the continued absence of effective government, ordinary people began to turn to the local "man of respect" with their questions and problems, thus increasing his power. Conflicts between men of respect themselves required the emergence of men of even greater respect to resolve them, and a loose, shifting hierarchy gradually evolved.

The unification of Italy enhanced rather than weakened the position of the Sicilian *mafiosi*. For the most part, the state virtually delegated its powers to them; the Mafia, after all, could be relied upon to deliver votes, and the politicians thus elected repaid them with suitable favors. "One hand washes the other," as the Italian saying has it. For the *mafiosi* it was a golden age. Soft-spoken bosses extorted whatever they wanted from the Sicilian economy and basked in respect.

The coming of Mussolini upset things for a while. The dictator could not countenance the challenge to his absolute power that the Mafia represented. Cesare Mori, the tough prefect sent to Palermo with orders to clean up Sicily, spelled out the new policy with brutal frankness: "If the Sicilians are afraid of the *mafiosi*, I'll convince them that I am the most powerful *mafioso* of them all." For a time, it seemed that Mori had almost eliminated the Mafia, but the cure was short-lived. Many of the *mafiosi* had sought exile in the United States, and in 1943 they were able to return to Sicily on the coattails of the United States Army. The Americans had planned to use the gangsters as a weapon of war against Mussolini, but the plan had unforeseen consequences. Mussolini's state vanished like a puff of smoke before the Allied onslaught; the returned *mafiosi* thrived.

In some ways, the Mafia found life in Italy after World War II very difficult. Emigration — both within Italy and across its borders — took away much of the population the Mafia had previously depended on, and the massive development of the south left many of the old-style bosses reeling with the same sort of culture shock that afflicted their more law-abiding compatriots.

The Mafia did not die out, however. It changed. By the 1970s, it and similar societies — the 'Ndrangheta of Calabria and the Camorra of Naples — had turned themselves into modern business enterprises, using criminal activities to finance more-or-less legitimate enterprises under their control. Among other things, they invested in enough heroin-producing equipment to provide an estimated 30 percent of American consumption. Naturally, it made good business sense to create a thriving home market for heroin, too: The Mafia has never allowed human misery to stand in its way.

The Mafia's transformation may in the long run prove to be its downfall. The old-style organization owed much of its strength to the essentially family loyalties on which it laid its foundations: The celebrated code of silence observed by its members, both in and out of police custody, was based on a perverted sense of honor as well as a straightforward fear of reprisal. Such loyalties are harder to engender in a Mafia in which computers and accountants seem almost more important than the old "men of respect" and, by offering immunities to informers, the Italian authorities have recently made headway against their oldest enemy. Nevertheless, according to a 1982 estimate, Italy's criminal economy — which is largely under Mafia control — was worth about 10 billion dollars. It is unlikely to disappear.

Whether the fabric of society can match the Mafia's resilience is a difficult question in Italy. Scorched by the forges of social change, seduced by consumerism and undermined by narcotics, in theory the Italian family should be approaching the status of an endangered species. Many Italians, in fact, are ready to declare the family extinct, even in the supposedly tradition-bound south.

"The old loyalties have disappeared," claims Luisa A. in Naples. "Everyone's out for himself. You even hear of people putting their parents into old folks' homes — we're as bad as the Milanese now."

"Once upon a time," explains a Tuscan restaurateur, "the family meant something. Now? Italian civilization's a joke. A new car, a washing machine — that's all they care about. No wonder the kids are killing themselves with drugs." "The Italian family?" asks a Milanese intellectual. "You've been watching too many old films. We're just another Western European country now — a few years behind the rest, maybe, but on the same road."

Interestingly, though, it is usually other people's families who are considered to have died out. Luisa, for example, returned from a lengthy stay in Milan at least in part because she wanted to be with her aging parents. The Tuscan's restaurant is entirely a family-run affair — and several times a week it is packed with vast, deafening, cheerful family parties. (They get together only

on special occasions these days, most of them explain; but they manage to find plenty of occasions special enough to justify holding a reunion.) And most Milanese, despite what some southerners may claim, would think it quite shameful to send their old folk into institutions — supposing the Italian state were ever to provide enough of them.

The Italian family, in short, may not be the unshakable foundation that it once was; but it has held out far better than its equivalents elsewhere. Indeed, not all of the changes have worked against the family. Traditionally, for instance, children lived at home with their parents until they were married. In the 1960s they were infected by Anglo-Saxon notions of breaking away, but today a chronic housing shortage is once more forcing children to stay at home until their wedding day, and sometimes even after it.

If Italians manage to hold on to their family way of life, they may be better placed than other nations to face the challenge of a rapidly changing future. The already dawning electronic age and the imminent information explosion promise to decentralize dramatically the means of wealth production. In such circumstances, Italy's lack of strong government could be an advantage, not a crippling defect, and all those resourceful, mutually supportive families could turn out to be a national asset that more disciplined nations will come to envy.

Italians who are living today, in the mid-1980s, have seen their country survive one dramatic transformation. If need be, they can survive another. They are not invulnerable to chaos and crisis, but they have learned to live with them. They may yet have to teach the rest of Europe how it is done. □

In Rome, one nun teaches housing-project children a song *(top)*, and another lends a supporting arm to an elderly woman on a stroll beside the Venetian lagoon *(above)*. All over Italy, those in need find a second family in the Roman Catholic Church, which performs many social services.

SUNDAY: THE PLEASURE OF SOCIALIZING

For the gregarious Italians, Sundays are, above all, an opportunity for sociability. Unlike nationalities for whom the day of rest means peace and quiet or the single-minded pursuit of a hobby, Italians at leisure consider that the greatest pleasure is to pass the time in the company of friends and relations. Family parties gather for lunch in seaside cafés or country *trattorie,* stretching the meal out for half the afternoon. Old men while away the hours around café tables. Young people flock together to flirt in groups that constantly dissolve and re-form. Sometimes the entertainment is on a less intimate scale, because throughout the length and breadth of the peninsula, Sunday is also the day for the nation's favorite mass spectator sport — soccer. The enthusiasts who crowd in to watch the matches enjoy taking part in the spectacle, with flamboyant demonstrations of support for local teams.

Such is their appetite for company that Italians can turn the most unpromising events into social occasions. A Sunday-morning visit to a cemetery, for instance, often takes on a neighborly air as mourners address themselves to the other visitors — and sometimes also to the dead. Even traffic jams can provide a certain camaraderie: Finding themselves in the company of other people and with time to kill, what else should the frustrated motorists do but get acquainted?

Appearing to pay a social call on their departed relatives, families crowd a cemetery in southern Italy's Basilicata region on All Saints' Day, when the dead are remembered. As on all Sundays and Holy Days, there are mourners who have come to address their thoughts to the deceased.

Steadied by many hands, a fan at a soccer match manipulates a heavy banner in an energetic exhibition of strength and skill.

Drivers caught in a summer-weekend traffic jam between Florence and the sea chat and wait philosophically.

On a Sunday evening in the little river-side town of Dolo near Padua, a handful of couples of widely differing ages dance on the stone terrace of a neighborhood café. At the tables, families converse in the warm dusk.

A family lingers over a midday meal on a Rimini beach. Before noon and later in the day, the beach is packed with family groups, but at lunchtime most retire to nearby restaurants.

Flocks of locals on the Venetian island
of Pellestrina watch as a fisherman
attempts a traditional feat of skill and
daring. His aim is to make his way
along a greased spar and reach the flag.

Relaxed young people while away the afternoon in the plaza of Forte dei Marmi, a seaside resort in Tuscany that has become their Sunday meeting place. They come on their motorcycles and mopeds from all over the region to enjoy one another's company.

Outside a tavern in Sacile, a small town in the northeast of Italy, elderly men linger over glasses of wine beneath signs offering sandwiches for sale. Their wives remain at home, preparing Sunday dinner.

A HISTORY OF DIVERSITY

Italy became a political entity little more than a century ago. Between the time of the collapse of the Roman Empire in the fifth century A.D. and the unification of Italy in 1861, no ruler was able to completely control the peninsula, although some tried. Italy was, as the Austrian statesman Metternich remarked in 1849, merely a "geographical expression."

Foreign powers dominated Italy for much of this period. During the Middle Ages, however, scores of Italian towns were able to govern themselves and their surrounding countryside with hardly any outside interference. The city-states developed strong local loyalties that remained a potent force even after unification. In the 20th century, the dictator Mussolini fanned nationalism by harking back to the Roman Empire. Since World War II, remarkable economic progress has given Italians a new and genuine pride in their nation. But because of a fragmented history, local affections still find as large a space as national allegiance in most Italians' hearts.

Before the Romans engulfed it, the Italian peninsula was, in common with the rest of Europe, divided like a checkerboard between tribal groups representing a variety of ethnic strains. Some peoples were of Mediterranean origin; others had moved across the Alps from central and northern Europe. By the eighth century B.C., they numbered among them two civilizations — one

A detail from the continuous frieze of Trajan's Column shows Roman legionnaires presenting the emperor with the severed heads of soldiers from vanquished Dacia — now Rumania. The marble monument was built in 114 A.D. to record Trajan's military career.

and possibly both of them imported — vastly more complex than the rest. The city-states of Greece had founded thriving colonies in Sicily and along the coast of southern Italy; and in central Italy, the Etruscans had emerged as an artistic and vigorous trading people. The Etruscan language was quite different from those of the other tribes in Italy, and according to one theory, the people originated in Asia Minor.

At the time the Etruscans began to flourish in Italy, Rome was no more than a well-used ford near the mouth of the Tiber River. But in the sixth century B.C., Etruscan colonists subjugated the local people — the Latin tribes — and a great city was developed.

For almost a century, Etruscan kings ruled Rome and the surrounding towns and countryside. They gave their subjects their alphabet, derived from that of the Greeks, and many of their religious and cultural practices. But the city's language remained Latin. At the end of the sixth century B.C., the Latins overthrew their Etruscan kings, and the new Roman republic that established itself emerged as the natural leader of the city-states of Latium.

Over the next 200 years, republican Rome gained control of central Italy, absorbing its friends and destroying its enemies. In the south, the Greek colonists retained their autonomy as allies of Rome, but they were later annexed. The republic's strength was its army, which had the incalculable advantage

41

of organization, against which enemies could muster only brute force and raw courage. The army's discipline was harsh. Cowards were flogged to death; disobedience by officers or men was punishable by beheading; thieves and deserters had their right hands cut off.

The basic Roman fighting unit, the legion, comprised 4,200 infantrymen, 300 cavalrymen and various supporting elements. The legion's backbone was the infantry, which was drawn up in three lines for battle. The first line discharged short throwing spears, then rushed forward to engage in hand-to-hand combat with short swords; if it failed to repel the enemy, the second line repeated the same sequence and the third line, armed with long spears, formed a reserve.

Pressing northward in the third and second centuries B.C., the Romans es-tablished their hegemony as far as the southern slopes of the Alps. As its sway expanded, Rome produced a succession of superb civil engineers who knitted the republic's conquered territories together by means of a network of roads. Some of the earliest of these highways, made of polygonal blocks of tufa carefully fitted together on a bed of gravel, are still in existence and have withstood centuries of use.

The conquest of Italy presented few serious obstacles, but during the third century B.C., Rome fought two prolonged and costly wars against Carthage, which was then the dominant sea power of the western Mediterranean. In the year 218 B.C., the great Carthaginian leader Hannibal succeeded in bringing an army equipped with war elephants across the Mediterranean, through Spain and over the Alpine passes into Italy. Although he devastated much of the open country, his forces proved to be no match for the rugged, indestructible Roman infantry, and Hannibal was forced to sue for peace.

The defeat of Carthage opened the way to still more extensive Roman conquests, from North Africa to England, and from Spain to Syria. The Mediterranean became a Roman lake — *mare nostrum,* or "our sea." There were Roman colonies along the Rhine and the Danube, and Roman governors in Athens and Alexandria. At home, the city of Rome itself grew into a metropolis of more than one million inhabitants and was known far and wide as *caput mundi,* the capital of the world.

Meanwhile, discontent was growing in the Italian countryside. One grievance voiced by the populace was that imports of foreign grain undermined

Italian agriculture, another that the immense fortunes won in distant corners of the empire were creating a gulf between rich and poor.

The first century B.C. was marked by civil war and insurrection, which the republican government was unable to contain. In 73 B.C., the Thracian slave Spartacus escaped with 70 others from a school for gladiators and quickly gathered an army of 70,000 runaway slaves, disaffected peasants and bandits. For two years, Spartacus harried the countryside and outmaneuvered the legions sent against him, until he was slain in the mountains of Calabria.

Two decades later, some of the generals of the Roman armies began plotting against the authority of the state. Julius Caesar, the brilliant strategist who had conquered Gaul — present-day France — revolted against the republic in 49 B.C., when he and one of his legions crossed the frontier into Italy in direct contravention of Roman law. After defeating his rival, Pompey, he crushed other insurgents in Asia Minor with his usual efficiency; his ruthless style made all the more impressive by the lapidary brevity of his dispatches from the field. *"Veni, vidi, vici"* — "I came, I saw, I conquered" — he wrote in the letter announcing the victory at Zela, where he defeated a Persian vassal. Soon after, he had himself declared dictator for life, but in 44 B.C., his career was cut short by the daggers of his enemies Brutus and Cassius.

After another struggle for power, Caesar was succeeded by his grand-nephew Octavian, who styled himself Caesar Augustus and established a new imperial order, in which Rome and its possessions were ruled by an all-powerful emperor. His successors on the throne continued to be known as

Caesar. Although their despotism produced a predictable upsurge of internal corruption, the empire itself continued to expand. By the second century of the Christian era — as Edward Gibbon remarks on the opening page of his marathon history, *The Decline and Fall of the Roman Empire* — the territory ruled by Rome "comprehended the fairest part of the earth, and the most civilized portion of mankind."

Never before had so many nations lived at peace with one another. From Libya to Britain and Godes (Cadiz) to Armenia there was one official language; one codified body of civil and criminal law; one system of coinage, of weights and measures, of government administration, of reckoning time.

Although Rome set the style in most things, it also absorbed the myriad cultural influences provided by its diverse provinces. Greek teachers instructed the Romans in science, philosophy and literature; Greek sculptors furnished the prototypes of Roman statues.

At the same time, the influx of easterners into Rome created new stan-

A marble head of Constantine I — sculpted for a 39-foot-tall statue a few years before his death in 337 A.D. — reveals the stern piety of a convert. Constantine, first Christian emperor of Rome, built churches, commissioned Bibles and abolished crucifixion.

dards of opulence and physical well-being. The *thermae,* or public baths — their walls covered with marble and mosaics, their waters flowing from silver taps into marble basins — became the center of social life. Men of wealth spent all afternoon at the baths, lounging in the courtyards or listening to the poets and declaimers who recited in the lecture rooms; adjoining gymnasiums had facilities for sports and ball games.

From the eastern provinces came mystery cults that supplemented and eventually supplanted the Roman state religion, with its pantheon headed by Jupiter, Juno and Minerva. These cults — promising the faithful life after death — helped to prepare the ground for Christianity, which reached Rome during the first century.

The early Christians were alternately tolerated and cruelly persecuted by the imperial authorities. For more than two centuries, their faith remained an underground movement. Early in the fourth century, however, the Emperor Constantine was converted to Christianity. In a series of edicts, he declared the pagan religions to be mere *superstitio* and made Christianity the state religion of Rome, thus giving the Church the new and unaccustomed role of being one of the main supports of imperial policy.

Politically and militarily, however, the empire was already in disarray. Barbarian armies from the north and east had overrun its outlying defenses and had pillaged such cities as Antioch and Lugdunum (Lyons). Under this onslaught, the government was decentralized, since it was impossible for one ruler to control the widely scattered imperial armies. In 330, Constantine removed the seat of empire from Rome to Byzantium, on the Bosphorus,

A work by the great painter-biographer Giorgio Vasari shows the army of the Holy Roman Emperor Charles V besieging Florence in 1529. With Michelangelo acting for a time as director of its fortifications, the city held out for a year before surrendering.

where he established a new capital city called Constantinople. In 395, the empire split into two parts, each with its own emperor; Ravenna became the capital of the western section.

But the new arrangement failed to protect Italy. In the first decade of the fifth century, Rome was sacked by the armies of Alaric the Visigoth. When this invasion was followed by that of other Germanic tribes, notably the Huns, the end was a foregone conclusion. In 476, the last titular emperor of the west, a young boy named Romulus Augustulus, was deposed by the Danubian general Odoacer, who ruled for 13 years as the first barbarian king of Italy — nominally under the aegis of the emperor of the east.

Although the Byzantine emperors made sporadic efforts to reassert their authority in Italy, their forces were no match for the various local powers that divided up the peninsula during the centuries that followed. Sicily, captured by Byzantium in the sixth century, did retain its allegiance to the eastern empire until the ninth century, and there were imperial officials in Calabria until the 11th century. But in the north, Teutonic invaders known as the Lombards established independent duchies, while in central Italy the popes — the bishops of Rome who were gradually becoming universally accepted as the spiritual leaders of Christendom — became temporal rulers.

The popes had acquired their territory by opposing Lombard expansion southward into Byzantine territory. In an attempt to contain their enemies, the popes called for assistance from the kings of the Franks (French), who by the eighth century had become the most powerful rulers north of the Alps.

First Pepin and then his son Charlemagne descended into Italy and fought victorious campaigns. They gave the papacy the lands that the Lombards had wrested from Byzantium — a belt crossing Italy diagonally from Ravenna to Rome — and retained the territories to the north for themselves.

Meanwhile, Charlemagne had conquered or allied himself with all the tribes of Germany and forcibly baptized any who were pagan. For his achievement in unifying the greater part of western Christendom, he was crowned Roman Emperor by Pope Leo III at the altar of St. Peter's Basilica in Rome on Christmas Day, 800.

The alliance between the pope and Charlemagne led to the establishment of the Holy Roman Empire — an empire that existed in theory rather than in practice, as the political expression of the medieval idea of a universal Christian empire. The pope was to be guardian of its spiritual values, and a temporal Caesar, drawn from the ranks of the northern kings, would act as defender of the faith. In name, at least, this shadowy empire survived for 1,000 years. It served primarily as a mantle of legitimacy for the titular emperors of Germany and Austria, who inherited Charlemagne's epithet when his line died out. They reigned as Holy Roman Emperors until the title was abolished by Napoleon in 1806.

Whatever its implications for the rest of Europe, the Holy Roman Empire was to have far-reaching effects on Italian history. By granting the popes temporal power over central Italy, the Holy Roman Empire served to cut off the north from the south, and thus divided the peninsula into three mutually suspicious zones. In addition, it linked the fate of Italy with that of Germany and Austria, providing an open door to foreign interference in Italian affairs.

Although the popes continued to crown the emperors, relations between the two powers deteriorated sharply after Charlemagne's reign: The ensuing centuries saw them locked in a bitter struggle for the control of Italy. The populace split into two parties, papalist and imperialist, which assumed the names of Guelph and Ghibelline respectively. Often one town would be torn by rivalry between the two sides.

But during the first part of the 12th century, a succession of emperors showed little interest in the affairs of

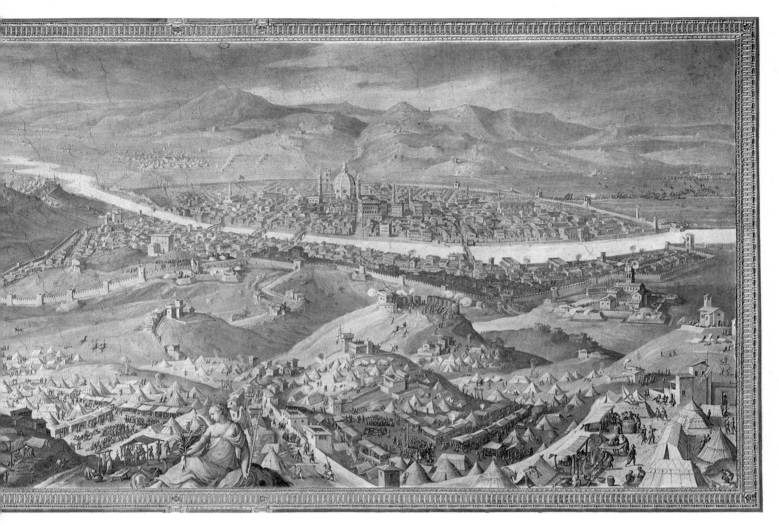

Italy. Many cities took advantage of the lull in outside interference to usurp the imperial powers. By the end of the century, a large part of Italy had become a mosaic of miniature republics, each consisting of a city and its surrounding countryside. The republics continued to jealously guard their autonomy after the emperors renewed their attentions. Even in areas with a monarchical style of government, such as the Papal States, cities enjoyed a good deal of autonomy. The communes proved fertile ground for new ideas, artistic movements and commercial ventures.

In the early years of the independent city-states, government in theory resided in the whole body of the citizens; in practice, however, only the more prominent members of the community normally participated. Subsequently, personal rule by a strong leader became more common, though the forms of a republic were often maintained. By the late 14th century, when both popes and emperors at last desisted from interfering in the communes' affairs, despotic dynasties had installed themselves almost everywhere.

The Tuscan city of Florence was one of the wealthiest of the communes. Wool was the source of its prosperity; the cloth woven there was known and sold throughout Europe. By the 14th century, Florence was a city of about 100,000 inhabitants and had 110 churches, 39 monasteries and convents. The more than 200 shops belonging to the wool merchants' guild annually produced cloth valued at 1.2 million florins — the florin being a highly prized gold coin first minted in the republic in 1252.

The money of the merchant class eventually eroded the power of the nobility. The city's government, although nominally republican, was essentially an oligarchy administered by and for

A CHRONOLOGY OF KEY EVENTS

c. 1000 B.C. Iron-age culture spreads throughout the Italian peninsula, which is inhabited by many different tribes speaking diverse languages.

750-550 B.C. Greek city-states found colonies in Sicily and southern Italy. Phoenicians from Carthage colonize western Sicily and Sardinia.

750-600 B.C. The Etruscans, a people of uncertain origin, spread through Tuscany, Lazio and Campania. They invent the arch and the vault and create sculptures in clay *(above)* and bronze.

750 B.C. Foundation of Rome.

750-510 B.C. Legendary period of the seven kings of Rome; the fifth and seventh are Etruscan.

509 B.C. The Romans overthrow their foreign rulers and set up a republic.

348-269 B.C. In stages, the Romans conquer or ally themselves with all the peoples of central and southern Italy.

264-241 B.C. The Romans wage the First Punic War against Carthage. The Romans annex Sicily, Sardinia and Corsica, the first of many overseas provinces.

218-201 B.C. The Carthaginian leader Hannibal starts the Second Punic War by invading Italy via Gaul and the Alps. The Romans are victorious, and take much of Spain from the Carthaginians.

58-44 B.C. The great Roman general Julius Caesar conquers Gaul. In a bid for power, Caesar returns to Italy with his army against the government's instructions. Civil war ensues. Caesar, victorious, becomes dictator in 47 B.C. Three years later, he is assassinated.

27 B.C.-14 A.D. Julius Caesar's adopted son Augustus *(above, being crowned by Victory)* reigns as Rome's first emperor. The whole Italian peninsula is incorporated into the Roman state. Rome now rules the entire Mediterranean world; the city is rebuilt with the appropriate grandeur.

40-100 Christianity spreads through the eastern part of the empire and reaches Rome.

79 Vesuvius erupts; Pompeii *(below)* and Herculaneum are destroyed.

117 The Roman Empire reaches its greatest size, stretching from the Caspian Sea to the Atlantic and from Britain to Egypt.

313-337 The Emperor Constantine makes Christianity the official religion of the empire. The western part of the empire is in economic decline and Constantine builds a new capital, Constantinople, in the east.

381 The bishop of Rome claims pre-eminence over other Christian bishops and assumes the title "Papa" — Father.

395 The empire is split in two. Constantinople remains the capital of the eastern empire; Ravenna becomes the capital of the western empire.

395-476 Waves of invaders from northern and central Europe weaken the western empire. In 476 the barbarian chief Odoacer deposes the western Roman emperor and rules Italy in his stead.

c. 529 Saint Benedict, a native of Umbria, formulates the rules that will govern monastic life in western Europe.

535-555 Justinian, emperor of the east, invades Italy and topples the barbarians from power. Italy becomes an outlying province of the eastern empire.

568 The Lombards, a Germanic people, enter Italy. In the next few years they conquer much of it. The eastern empire retains Sicily, the far south of the peninsula, and a band across Italy from Ravenna to Rome.

732-756 The Lombards encroach on Ravenna and Rome. Pope Stephen II invites Pepin, the king of France, to attack the Lombards. Pepin forces the Lombards out of their newly conquered territories; instead of returning these lands to the eastern empire, he gives them to the pope. This marks the beginning of the Papal States.

774 Pepin's son Charlemagne defeats the Lombards and rules over their lands in Italy. He confirms the pope's right to govern the band of territory between Ravenna and Rome.

800 Charlemagne, now ruler of much of western Europe, is crowned Holy Roman Emperor by Pope Leo III.

827-878 Arabs conquer Sicily and the southern mainland. Under their rule, the area prospers and intellectual life flourishes.

1030-1137 Normans conquer Sicily and southern Italy, and they establish an efficient rule.

1100-1200 Scores of northern cities, theoretically under the rule of the Holy Roman Emperor or the eastern emperor, become virtually self-governing.

1204-1472 Venice acquires a great overseas empire, which includes Crete, Cyprus and the Dalmatian coast.

1209 Saint Francis of Assisi *(below)* founds an order of mendicant friars.

1220-1250 Inheriting the Holy Roman Empire from his father and Sicily, with southern Italy, from his Norman mother, Frederick II of Hohenstaufen reigns gloriously in the south but fails to impose his authority on the northern communes.

1266 A French prince, Charles of Anjou, takes over southern Italy and Sicily at the invitation of the pope.

1271 Marco Polo embarks from Venice on a 24-year-long journey through the Far East.

1282 In an uprising known as the Sicilian Vespers, the Sicilians revolt against the French and bestow the crown of Sicily on the Spaniard Peter of Aragon.

1305 A French pope, Clement V, transfers the seat of the papacy to Avignon, where it will remain for 72 years.

1348 The bubonic plague kills one third of the population of Italy.

1434 Cosimo de'Medici *(above)* gains power in Florence. He and his successors patronize the artists and philosophers of the Renaissance.

1442 The French line ruling southern Italy dies out, and the Spanish king of Sicily wins control of the southern mainland.

1494 Charles VIII of France, pretender to the crown of southern Italy, invades the peninsula. Piero de'Medici, ruler of Florence, cooperates with the

1350-1454 During a century of warfare, the communes of Florence, Venice *(above)* and Milan swallow up other city-states. By 1454, when the Peace of Lodi is agreed, Italy consists of five major states and a few minor ones.

1360 The Tuscan-born poet Francesco Petrarca (Petrarch) publishes his lines addressed to Laura, an idealized beloved. In his aim — the enrichment of the human mind and conscience — he prefigures the Renaissance, and his verses will have a strong influence on European poetry for centuries.

enemy and is driven out of the city. The friar Savonarola sets up a short-lived republic in Florence. The French take southern Italy but by 1496 the Spaniards have driven them out.

1503 Julius II becomes pope and makes Rome the center of High Renaissance art and learning.

1525-1559 Spain gains control of most of northern Italy.

1545-1563 The Council of Trent, the key event in the Counter Reformation, clarifies Catholic doctrine and decrees reforms in the clergy.

1613 Galileo, the first scientist to use a telescope *(below),* produces evidence that the earth revolves around the sun.

1713 Spain is weakened by war and most of her Italian possessions — notably Milan and the south — are acquired by Austria. Sicily is handed to the Duke of Savoy, ruler of French Savoy and Italian Piedmont.

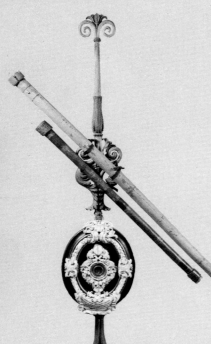

1720 The Duke of Savoy exchanges Sicily for the Kingdom of Sardinia.

1734 Spain retakes southern Italy and Sicily.

1796-1799 The French Revolutionary army, led by Napoleon, conquers Italy and sets up a number of republics modeled on the French one. An Austrian offensive and nationalist risings force the French to withdraw from Italy by 1799.

1800-1814 Napoleon reconquers Italy. In 1805, he bestows on himself the crown of Italy *(right);* by 1809, the whole peninsula is ruled directly or indirectly from France. The French introduce a modern legal system and improve the administration.

1815 At the Congress of Vienna, held after Napoleon's downfall, Italy is re-

partitioned among its former rulers. A branch of the Spanish Bourbon dynasty is reinstated in the south, the pope retains the center, Austria most of the

north, and the king of Sardinia, Piedmont.

1832 The exiled revolutionary Giuseppe Mazzini *(above)* founds Young Italy, a movement for national unity.

1848 A popular uprising in Palermo spreads to other areas; in response, liberal constitutions are granted in several states, including Piedmont. While Austria has internal rebellions, Venice and Milan free themselves.

1849 Following unrest in Rome and the flight of the pope, a republic is founded. The republican army, under Giuseppe Garibaldi, is defeated by French forces; the pope returns. Austria crushes rebellions in other states and repeals new constitutions everywhere except in Piedmont.

1859 Camillo Cavour, prime minister of Piedmont, makes a treaty with France to rid Italy of the Austrians.

1859 France defeats the Austrians at Magenta and Solferino. Austria loses Lombardy to the French, who cede it to Piedmont. The rulers of Parma, Modena and Tuscany — all Austrian satellite princes — flee Italy.

1860 In plebiscites held in Parma, Modena and Tuscany, the populations vote for unity with Piedmont. Revolutionaries in Sicily request Garibaldi's help. He embarks from Genoa with 1,100 volunteers. Garibaldi quickly takes Sicily in the name of Victor Emmanuel, the king of Sardinia and ruler of Piedmont, then crosses to the mainland. As he approaches Naples, the capital of the southern realm, its ruler flees. Meanwhile, the regular Piedmontese army annexes the Papal States. Italy is now almost united but the pope, supported by the French, retains Rome and its environs, and Austria keeps the northeast.

1861 Victor Emmanuel *(above)* becomes king of Italy. The constitution of Piedmont is used for the new nation, and Turin becomes the capital.

1866 After a war with Austria, Italy acquires the state of Venice.

1870 France, occupied with the Franco-Prussian War, withdraws troops from Rome. The Italian army marches on Rome and the pope surrenders. He is granted sovereignty over the Vatican City but refuses to recognize the new order. Rome becomes seat of national government.

1870-1914 More than 10 million Italians emigrate — mainly to other European countries, Brazil, Argentina and the United States.

1887-1896 Italy attempts to conquer Ethiopia, but is driven out.

1896-1900 Socialists promote disorder among Italians restive because of bad harvests and unemployment. Military rule is imposed in some areas.

1899 Giovanni Agnelli founds the auto-manufacturing company Fiat.

1909 Guglielmo Marconi, inventor of the wireless, receives a Nobel prize.

1912 Italy takes Libya from Turkey.

Alto Adige and Trieste. However, Dalmatia becomes part of Yugoslavia, and Fiume, an Italian-speaking city on the Croatian coast, becomes a Free Port. The poet Gabriele d'Annunzio, at the head of a band of fanatics, seizes control of Fiume and rules the city for more than a year.

1919-1921 Amid social and economic turbulence and discontent over the outcome of the war, Benito Mussolini forms bands of thugs known as *fasci di combattimento*. A weak coalition government stands back while the Fascists destroy the headquarters of the Socialist and Communist parties and break strikes.

1921 Mussolini and 34 other Fascists are elected to Parliament.

1922 After breaking a general strike, the Fascists seize key communication points, threatening to isolate Rome from the rest of the country. Victor Emmanuel III invites Mussolini to form a government.

1923 Mussolini devises a new electoral system that will ensure a huge Fascist majority, and Parliament accepts it.

1925-1926 Mussolini begins to rule openly as dictator.

1939 Mussolini and Hitler sign a military treaty, the Pact of Steel. World War II breaks out.

1940 Italy declares war on France and Britain.

1943 Allied armies land in Sicily. The Fascist regime collapses and Mussolini is arrested. In the south, a new Italian government controlled by the Allies declares war on Germany. Mussolini, freed by the Germans, establishes a rival government in the north.

1945 Mussolini is captured and shot by partisans. World War II ends.

1946 A popular referendum abolishes the monarchy.

1945-1953 Alcide de Gasperi, the leader of the Christian Democrat party, heads seven successive administrations.

1947 A new republican constitution is approved.

1950-1970 Italy industrializes rapidly, to become one of the seven largest economies in the world.

1978 Former prime minister Aldo Moro is kidnaped and murdered by the Red Brigades, culminating several years of terrorist attacks.

1981-1985 Giovanni Spadolini, leader of the Republican party, becomes the first non-Christian Democrat prime minister since 1945; he is followed in August 1983 by Bettino Craxi, the first Socialist to fill this role.

1914-1918 World War I breaks out. After Britain and France agree to back Italy's claims to the Trentino, the Alto Adige, Trieste and northern Dalmatia, Italy declares war on Austria in 1915 and on Germany in 1916. Italy suffers several defeats but in the final months of war makes a notable contribution to the Allied victory.

1919-1921 The peace treaty of World War I grants Italy the Trentino, the

1929 Mussolini concludes the Lateran Treaty with the papacy *(above)*. The pope at last recognizes the Kingdom of Italy; Catholicism is confirmed as the state religion.

1935 Italy attacks Ethiopia and in 1936 proclaims an Italian empire.

1936-1939 Italy and Germany support General Franco in the Spanish Civil War.

2

the merchants. The masters of the guilds regulated every detail of trade.

The wealth of Florence gave it an educated upper class that tended to expend its energies in political feuds between the Guelph and Ghibelline parties. The Ghibellines were eventually expelled and the Guelphs split into two factions, the Whites and the Blacks. But the elite also produced the first stirrings of the humanism that was to blossom into the Italian Renaissance: the revival of classical science and philosophy and of pagan themes in painting and sculpture. Dante Alighieri, the greatest Italian poet, was born in Florence in 1265 and had a thorough education in the Latin classics. The humanist scholar Leonardo Bruni wrote a century later, "by study of philosophy, theology, astrology, arithmetic and geometry, by reading history, by the turning over of many curious books, watching and sweating in his studies, he acquired the science that he was to adorn and explain in his verses."

Early in the 14th century, after the triumph of the Blacks over the Whites, Dante was banished from his native city with 600 others of the White party. He was never again to see the towers of Florence: Instead, he spent the rest of his life wandering from one northern city to the next, seeking the protection of such patrons as the ruler of Verona, Can Grande della Scala, to whom he dedicated the *Paradiso* section of his greatest work, the *Divine Comedy.* Dante's *Commedia* — the adjective *Divinia* was added by a 16th-century editor — includes brilliant passages of documentary reporting as well as complex religious allegories, all expressed in *terza rima,* resonant, melodic verse.

Dante died in Ravenna in 1321 after undertaking a diplomatic mission to Venice on behalf of the local ruler, Guido da Polenta. By then, Ravenna had lost its erstwhile importance as the seat of emperors; the principal city-state on the Adriatic coast was Venice — no more than a collection of fishermen's huts under the Romans, but now grown wealthy and impregnable, thanks to the vast fleet of cargo vessels and fighting galleys with which it dominated the eastern Mediterranean.

During the 13th century, Venice had despoiled the Byzantine empire of many Greek islands and of extensive territory along the coasts of the Adriatic and the Black Sea. A long and bitter rivalry with the maritime republic of Genoa came to a head in 1379, when the Genoese sent a fleet to blockade the Venetians in their own lagoon — only to be caught in a trap at Chioggia, on the southern edge of the lagoon, where the Genoese navy was forced to surrender. Genoa never recovered from this defeat, and Venice was left with uncontested mastery of the Mediterranean.

Venice, like Genoa, was a republic, but one of a curious sort. As the English writer James Morris put it, "Venice was a sort of police state, except that instead of worshipping power, she was terrified of it and refused it to any single one of her citizens." The governing body, the Council of Ten, controlled security agencies that were prepared to murder or imprison in order to prevent popular uprisings or personal dictatorship. The doge, or chief magistrate, though able to assume real powers in times of emergency, was otherwise a figurehead. Usually the choice fell on someone past his prime, who was kept a virtual prisoner within his glorious palace. In a great water festival held each year on Ascension Day, the doge would be rowed out to the mouth of the lagoon in his golden state barge, and there, after the sea had been blessed with holy water, he would throw in a ring and pronounce the time-hallowed formula: "In sign of eternal dominion, we, the doge of Venice, marry you, O sea!"

In the early 15th century, Venice consolidated its power by annexing the adjoining mainland states, including Padua, Vicenza and Verona. Soon afterward, the Venetians came into conflict with the dukes of Milan, who fought several bloody wars to prevent the republic of Venice from extending its frontiers into Lombardy.

This fertile, prosperous region had seen the establishment of European prototype banks in the 12th century; financiers from the city of Piacenza became so dominant in their profession that in northern Europe bankers and money lenders were known generically as "lombards." By the 14th century, Milan had become the foremost of the Lombard city-states. It proclaimed its affluence by erecting a series of churches and palaces that were more splendid than any other city's. The cathedral of Milan, begun in 1386, was designed to be the largest in the world, with space for 40,000 worshippers.

While the northern city-states competed and skirmished, the south was subjected to repeated invasions. Arabs conquered Sicily in the ninth century and then used the island as a base for expansion along the southern Italian coastline; Normans followed them two centuries later. Next, it was the turn of the Hohenstaufen dynasty of southern Germany and then of the Angevins of southwestern France. By the 15th century, the Spanish kings of Aragon were in control of Sicily and the southern Italian mainland, which now was known as the Kingdom of Naples.

The 15th century was a period of consolidation everywhere in Italy. Powerful city-states swallowed up the weaker ones, and by midcentury, most of Italy fell within one of five states: Milan, Venice, Florence, the Papal States and the southern kingdom. Venice remained a republic, but Milan was by now a duchy ruled by the Sforza family, and Florence's affairs were directed by the Medici dynasty. The popes set about centralizing the government of their territory and became increasingly important temporal rulers. The office of supreme pontiff came to be regarded as an exclusively Italian preserve. Between the mid-15th century and the late 20th century, only three non-Italians were elected to the Holy See by the College of Cardinals. Many of the most famous landmarks of Renaissance Rome were built by wealthy, worldly pontiffs who belonged to one or another of the great Italian families, such as the Medici, the Farnese and the Rovere.

In the 16th century, the papacy was increasingly beset by a revolt in the Christian ranks — the Protestant Reformation. To counteract the growing power of the Protestants in Germany, England, the Netherlands and Scandinavia, successive popes carried out a wide-ranging program of renewal, the Counter Reformation. Outward symbols of this policy included the refurbishing of Rome under Pope Sixtus V in the 1580s, when the Lateran Palace was restored, many streets and squares rebuilt, dozens of monuments erected — and the great basilica of St. Peter's received its dome. Sixtus' administrative reforms were equally thorough. In only five years as pontiff, as one historian of the papacy expressed it, the indefatigable Sixtus "laid the foundations of that wonderful and silent engine of universal government by which Rome still rules the Catholics of every land on the face of the globe."

The period of the Church's triumph saw the decline of Italy's independent states, as one after another fell under foreign domination. The foretaste of events came in 1494 when Charles VIII of France, claiming lordship over Naples and Milan, invaded Italy from the north. His campaign proved to be a failure, but the ease with which he was expelled lulled Italian rulers into a false sense of security. It became their habit to invite in foreign powers to further their personal political interests. Once entrenched, the allies proved impossible to oust. In the course of the 16th century, France did acquire some Italian territories but was driven out by Spain. Until the 18th century, the Hapsburg kings of Spain ruled large parts of Italy and maintained a protectorate over most of the rest. Venice and the Papal States were the only substantial Italian territories to retain their independence. Spanish rule encouraged corruption and also weakened initiative in a people already exhausted by war.

The death of the last Spanish Hapsburg in 1700 resulted in conflict on a European scale: The War of the Spanish Succession ended in 1713 with a young Bourbon king, a grandson of

A crowned figure of the Church Triumphant dominates a painting of the Council of Trent, the 16th-century conference of bishops that launched the Counter Reformation. The council promoted ecclesiastical reforms and clarified disputed points of doctrine.

A HERO OF TWO WORLDS

Giuseppe Garibaldi, the romantic hero of Italian unification, was born in 1807 in Nice, which became part of Piedmont when he was seven. A passionate idealist at 26, he met confederates of Giuseppe Mazzini, the exiled theorist behind the Risorgimento, and vowed to work for Italian unity. Soon afterward, he took part in an unsuccessful republican plot against the Piedmont dynasty and had to flee to South America.

In exile, Garibaldi acquired formidable military skills — first as a sea captain, then as a guerrilla leader fighting for any cause he considered just. In that unruly continent, where every man was a law unto himself, Garibaldi inspired his troops by the sheer force of his personality — his courage, honesty and simplicity.

In 1848, Garibaldi returned to Italy to fight for its redemption. Twelve years later, he embarked on the military expedition for which he will always be remembered. Setting sail from Genoa with a band of 1,100 volunteers, he liberated Sicily and the southern mainland from their despotic ruler — uniting northern Italy with the south. The Italians revered Garibaldi, and when he was injured, scraps of his bloodied clothing were treasured as relics. When he died, in 1882, the former revolutionary was given a state funeral and mourned as a national hero.

A contemporary painting *(right, above)* **shows Garibaldi landing in Sicily in 1860 with the banner that became the flag of united Italy. The country's disunity is satirized by an 1866 cartoon** *(right):* **Figures representing the northern regions strive to join hands with the south across the Papal States.**

Louis XIV of France, enthroned in Madrid. In the interest of maintaining the balance of power in Europe between the Bourbons and the Hapsburgs of Austria, Italy was carved up anew. Most of the Spanish possessions passed to the Austrian Hapsburgs — who were, on the whole, more enlightened and progressive rulers than the Spaniards had been. They streamlined the administration and developed the economy of territories under their control. However, the reforms were limited in scope, and the Austrian overlords' minds were generally on matters other than Italy.

A minor beneficiary from the redistribution was Piedmont — a small independent buffer state between France and Milan — which gained Sicily. Such were the chess-game politics of the time that the great powers obliged Piedmont's ruler to exchange Sicily for Sardinia five years later. Not long afterward, the Spanish Bourbons occupied Sicily and the southern mainland.

With roughly 300,000 inhabitants, the city of Naples, the capital of their realm, was then the second most populous city in Europe, after Paris. Under the Bourbons it became famed for the sumptuousness of its immense royal palace and its opera house, as well as for the squalor of its back streets. The monarchy's richest agricultural land was owned by the king, the nobles and the Church. "If we divide all the families in the kingdom into 60 parts," wrote the priest and economics lecturer Abbé Antonio Genovesi in the 1760s, "one of these owns land and 59 have not sufficient to be buried in."

The French Revolution, which set out to redress such inequities, launched Italy on a fresh round of wars and massacres. In 1796, a republican army under General Napoleon Bonaparte in-

A painting portrays the carnage at Dogali, in Eritrea, where 500 Italians died in 1887. The Colony of Eritrea was officially proclaimed in 1890 by Premier Francesco Crispi, but the struggle for control over this territory continued for several years.

vaded Italy and drove the Austrians out of the north. In the wake of his victorious campaign, Napoleon left a string of hastily formed Italian republics based on the French model. Ironically, the one existing republic, Venice, was abolished by a Napoleonic stroke of the pen and handed over to Austria as part of a peace package.

Napoleon soon became embroiled in Egypt; with French troops unavailable to defend their new sphere of influence in Italy, retribution was swift and ruthless. In 1799, despots throughout the peninsula returned to their thrones and wreaked vengeance on the republicans. In the city of Naples, hundreds of supporters of the short-lived republic — mainly the young nobles and the city's intelligentsia — surrendered their arms to a monarchist army and an English fleet under Admiral Horatio Nelson, on the condition that they would be allowed to sail to France or return to their homes unmolested. Instead, they were condemned to execution or life imprisonment as galley slaves.

With Napoleon's return to Europe, the pendulum swung once more in the other direction. In 1800, Napoleon, who was now France's first consul, organized a new Italian campaign. By 1810, as emperor of France, he had a tenuous control — directly or indirectly — over the entire Italian peninsula: Piedmont, Tuscany and Rome were annexed to France; Venice and Milan formed the core of the Kingdom of Italy, ruled by Napoleon; and he installed his brother-in-law, Joachim Murat, as king of Naples.

In a decade or so of Napoleonic administration, many parts of Italy experienced their first taste of reasonably impartial, efficient government. Napoleon's officials brought energy and enthusiasm to provinces that had been demoralized by centuries of suffocating rule by foreign viceroys: Napoleon modernized the legal system, built new roads, bridges and schools, and trained regiments of soldiers in the latest fighting tactics. Moreover, because the French chose to ignore the old state boundaries, the inhabitants of the peninsula were encouraged to think of themselves as Italians rather than as Tuscans, Lombards, or whatever.

Napoleon's empire collapsed in 1814; the French withdrew from Italy and the absolutist regimes were reimposed at bayonet point. Their brutality and corruption made many people look back on the French occupation as a period of comparative freedom.

Thenceforth, the idea of Italian unity and independence increasingly attracted support among intellectuals, army officers, bureaucrats and a few nobles. A secret society known as the Carboneria — the charcoal burners, from whom the group took its name, spent much time working unseen in inaccessible forests — agitated for reforms in Naples and fomented revolutions in Parma, Modena and the Romagna, which were suppressed by force of Austrian arms.

When uncovered, members of the Carboneria were tortured, imprisoned and executed, but their fate failed to stamp out the freedom movement: Italian writers and composers began to engage in creating a subversive literature and even covertly nationalist operas that slipped through the tight net of Austrian censorship. For example, in

2

Giuseppe Verdi's 1842 opera *Nabucco,* he portrayed the Jews of the Old Testament in captivity in Babylon. Verdi conveyed their longing for deliverance in a moving chorus that the Italian public interpreted as their own prayer for liberation from the Austrian yoke. Giuseppe Mazzini, author of important works on Italian liberty and unity, spent most of his life in exile, rallying support for revolution.

In 1848, a year of unrest throughout all of Europe, Milan rose in revolt. The troops of Piedmont — which alone among the northern Italian states was independent of Austria — came to the defense of Milan's provisional government in what came to be known as the First War of Independence. After four months, the war ended in defeat for Piedmont. The Venetians tried to throw off Austrian rule at the same time, but were starved into surrender after a five-month siege. In Rome, revolutionaries declared a republic that accomplished much for the city's poor but alienated the Roman Catholic Church and the wealthier citizens. Pope Pius IX left the Quirinal Palace disguised as a priest and fled to Neapolitan territory, whence he appealed to the French for aid. Allied with Austria, Naples and Spain, France moved quickly to crush an army of 10,000 Roman volunteers led by the self-taught guerrilla fighter Giuseppe Garibaldi.

Despite Garibaldi's defeat, Il Risorgimento, or "The Revival," acquired what became an irresistible momentum. The prime minister of Piedmont and principal architect of Italian unification, Count Cavour, carefully orchestrated a new attack on Austria. This time, a treaty with Napoleon III of France secured him as his ally. In 1859, the French won two major victories against the Austrians in northern Italy, at Magenta and Solferino, and forced them to agree to an armistice. Louis Napoleon's aim had been to secure Savoy and Nice for France; once these objectives were attained, he left Peidmont to its own devices.

While Cavour's agents annexed Tuscany and Emilia to Piedmont by means of hastily organized plebiscites, Garibaldi mustered a force of 1,100 volunteers — known as "The Thousand" — to go to the aid of the Sicilians, who had revolted against Francis II of Naples but were on the point of being crushed by a Neapolitan army of 20,000. Garibaldi landed at Marsala in Sicily in May 1860, fought a campaign of surprise and deception against the army of occupation, and soon had the entire island firmly in his grasp. In mid-August, his irregulars crossed to the mainland and marched northward. Three weeks later, Francis II fled from Naples only a day before Garibaldi entered the city and found himself greeted as a liberator by cheering crowds.

The Piedmontese reacted by sending a royal army marching south through the Papal States, and defeated a thin screen of papal troops at Castelfidardo. At Teano, north of Naples, Garibaldi's forces linked up with the army headed by Victor Emmanuel, the ruler of Piedmont, who was proclaimed king of a united Italy in March 1861. His capital, Turin, became the first capital of the country.

Only Venice and the rump Papal States still remained outside the borders of the new kingdom, the former to be ceded by Austria in 1866, the latter to be annexed in 1870, when the Italian army entered Rome following the withdrawal of the city's French garrison. A plebiscite confirmed the Romans' overwhelming support for unity with Italy. At last the nation could move its seat of government to the city that was its logical capital.

One cloud hanging over united Italy was the implacable hostility of the pope, shorn of almost all his temporal powers. A law was passed recognizing the pope as an independent sovereign within the Vatican, the enclave of Rome encompassing St. Peter's and the headquarters of the Catholic Church. But Pius IX persisted in regarding himself as "the prisoner of the Vatican." He refused to treat with the new government and imposed a ban designed to prevent practicing Catholics from voting in parliamentary elections.

There were additional reasons for the people of Italy to be less than fully committed to the new state. The regime was a constitutional monarchy with freedom of the press and without a secret police, but it had a highly centralized structure modeled on that of France, which was manifestly inappropriate for a nation with strong regional loyalties. Its constitution debarred illiterates from voting — not too serious an obstacle for Italians in the north, but for the south a barrier that disenfranchised more than 80 percent of the voting-age population. Understandably, farmers and laborers felt that they had no stake in the government; the south had exchanged an inefficient feudal government by Spanish agents for an unresponsive government by northern Italian bureaucrats, who understood it no better.

The first decades of Italian unity failed to achieve any dramatic gains internally, and successive governments tried to foster a sense of national purpose by means of foreign conquests. In

Mussolini wears the stony mask he assumed when listening to parliamentary speeches.

Il Duce wields a shovel in a propaganda exercise to show him as a man of the people.

"I made my own rules and I did not keep even them," declared Benito Mussolini, and that cynical boast could serve as an epitaph for a man who was less a statesman than an actor.

Born in 1883, the son of a socialist blacksmith and a devout Catholic schoolteacher, he was expelled from one school and suspended from another for stabbing fellow students. He later completed his education but showed little intellectual promise. Between 1902 and 1919 he was a teacher, bohemian, socialist agitator, soldier and journalist before he launched the fascist movement and promoted it through his newspaper.

After he became dictator of Italy in the mid-1920s, he devoted his energy to the quest for adulation, using propaganda to convince the people that he was, in his words, "the greatest personality in Europe." Claiming that he worked a 19-hour day almost singlehandedly running the state, he left his study lights burning at night while he regularly slept nine hours. Parliament survived only as a theater for his spellbinding oratory, and reports of debates were sometimes altered to fit the requirements of publicity. Obsessed with physical prowess, he was always willing to show off his manly jaw and barrel chest for photographers, and at public meetings he concealed his shortness by standing on a stool. To demonstrate his vigor, he took to reviewing military parades at a run, a comic-opera effect heightened by his extravagant uniforms.

Although Mussolini was well aware of Italy's military limitations, his envy of Hitler's conquests drove him to emulate the man he had once dismissed as a "silly little clown." After Mussolini was deposed in July of 1943, he spent much of his last two years "thinking only of history and how he would appear in it."

2

the 1880s and 1890s, following the example of the large European powers, Italy attempted to establish colonies in East Africa, but its forces were repeatedly defeated by the Ethiopians and Italy was able to colonize only Eritrea. Italy entered World War I on the side of the Allies in 1915 in the hope of acquiring Italian-speaking territories in Austria and of obtaining concessions in Africa, the Middle East and the eastern Mediterranean, where the Turkish empire was on the point of collapse. In a secret agreement signed in 1915, Britain and France acceded to almost all of Italy's territorial demands. But the war proved far more costly than anyone had anticipated: Italy mobilized 5.2 million men, of whom more than 600,000 lost their lives in a long, bloody stalemate on the Austrian front. At the peace table, Italy received large Austrian territories but failed to obtain the other territories it aspired to in Africa and the Balkans.

Disillusioned and impoverished, postwar Italy was ripe for new kinds of political adventurism. For 16 months in 1919 and 1920, the swashbuckling poet Gabriele d'Annunzio and a band of ragtag followers occupied the port of Fiume, in Croatia, whose predominantly Italian population was fearful of being absorbed into the newly created nation of Yugoslavia.

D'Annunzio's posturings and pretensions may have served as examples to Benito Mussolini, an accomplished orator who organized the black-shirted Fascist movement of the right as a counterweight to the rising influence of the Communists on the left of the political spectrum. Many of the Fascisti were street toughs with war experience, hostile to intellectuals and revolutionary workers but not averse to political

upheaval. Mussolini attracted followers with a vague, patriotic philosophy: He professed to be on the side of the poor, of social reform and national awakening — a mixture of platitudes that had not been tried elsewhere in Europe.

When the Italian Socialists called a general strike in August 1922, the Fascists claimed that public order was in jeopardy and seized control of the transportation and communications systems; they were soon running essential services themselves. At the end of October, Fascist battalions threatened to enter Rome. Mussolini — now leader of the 35 Fascist deputies in Parliament — hurried from Milan and was appointed premier by a thoroughly intimidated King Victor Emmanuel III.

Within three years, Mussolini had effectively short-circuited parliamentary democracy and had also assumed dictatorial powers. All opposition was silenced, by force if necessary. In 1924, the young Socialist leader Giacomo Matteotti, who had tried to have the recent election results declared invalid, was kidnaped and stabbed to death. Mussolini denied any association with the crime, but it was clear that the murderers were carrying out his wishes. Beginning with such arbitrary acts of violence, the Fascists soon succeeded in turning Italy into a well-organized police state. Political opponents of the regime were imprisoned or murdered, and civil rights were suppressed.

Initially, Mussolini had no coherent political program and considered it an advantage: There would be fewer reasons for opposition. Later, he introduced a planned economy and involved the state in all aspects of life, from education and sports to industry and trade. In 1929, his government negotiated the Lateran Treaty with the

Vatican. The Catholic Church — for a large sum of money and acknowledgment as the official religion — at last recognized the Italian state.

As Il Duce (The Leader), Mussolini made earnest attempts to unite the population by such means as the prohibition of regional dialects and the standardization of the school curriculum. A vast propaganda machine glossed over the regime's crimes and errors and whipped up popular enthusiasm for its achievements, including a crackdown on the Sicilian Mafia, the draining of the malaria-ridden Pontine marshes near Rome and — the feat most often quoted by foreigners — "making the trains run on time." In 1935, Europe watched with alarm and amazement when Mussolini sent an expeditionary force to Ethiopia: Italian poison gas and machine guns made short work of an Ethiopian militia armed with spears and shotguns. It was said that Mussolini had revived the glories of the Roman Empire: Whenever he made a public appearance, he was greeted by ecstatic crowds chanting *"Du-ce! Du-ce!"*

But Mussolini's Ethiopian adventure served to estrange him from Britain and France, and propelled him into the orbit of Europe's other leading dictator, Adolf Hitler. The Rome-Berlin Axis established in 1936 fatally entangled Italian imperialism with the far more virulent belligerence of Nazi Germany. In June 1940, Mussolini led his country into World War II on the side of Germany and divided public opinion as never before. Three million Italians were conscripted into the armed forces to fight, often reluctantly, on the German side.

By 1943, the Axis had clearly outlived its usefulness; Hitler's armies had reached their high-water mark and

were in retreat in the Soviet Union and North Africa, where their Italian allies had been forced to share their defeat. That summer, the British and American forces landed in Sicily. In July, while the Allies overran Sicily, dissident Fascists — supported by the king and Italy's High Command — deposed Il Duce. In September, the king and the army asked for an armistice; later the provisional government reversed alliances and declared war on Germany. Hitler's forces, however, rescued Mussolini, reinforced their defensive positions in the north and set up a puppet regime, the "Italian Social Republic." After a long campaign, in which Italian

partisans played a considerable role, the Germans finally surrendered in the spring of 1945. Mussolini was captured and killed by partisans when he tried to escape with the fleeing Germans.

The Italian monarchy had been discredited by its acceptance, albeit reluctant, of the Fascist dictatorship. In a June 1946 referendum, 12.7 million Italians voted for a republic, and 10.7 million preferred the monarchist status quo. The royal family went into exile and the Republic of Italy was declared. In 1947, a new constitution was adopted. Italy became a member of the North Atlantic Treaty Organization (NATO) in 1949 and was a founding

member of the European Economic Community (EEC) when it was established in 1957.

Even before World War II was over, Italy had learned its lesson from the catastrophic failure of authoritarianism. Back in the democratic mainstream, and freed from Mussolini's absurdly wasteful imperialism, postwar Italy quickly caught up with levels of culture and rates of economic progress that prevailed elsewhere in Europe. Success bred new confidence and optimism within the country and enhanced its standing abroad. Once more, the nation took its place as a highly respected member of the world community. □

Cans of paint and aerosol sprays sur-
round a marble niche and sculpture in
an 18th-century Carrara mansion
that has become a hardware shop. As
the town's most plentiful raw material,
marble is used in buildings both
luxurious and plain, providing everything from floors to tabletops.

CARRARA: MARBLE CAPITAL OF THE WORLD

For 2,000 years, the men of Carrara have cut the world's most precious white stone from the Apuane Alps, peaks of solid marble that encircle the Tuscan town. The original quarry may have provided cladding for the monuments of imperial Rome. Renaissance sculptors prized Carrara's product for its snowy purity and compact grain; Michelangelo often climbed the rock walls around the town in search of flawless pieces. Today, Carrara's river runs white with dust from the approximately one million tons of marble cut annually, most of it destined to become architectural slabs or tombstones.

The marble workers of Carrara and the surrounding towns have handed down their skills through the generations. With the precision of diamond cutters, the quarriers split massive slabs away from the rock face. In the mills where the stone is cut and polished, craftsmanship is so fine that countries as distant as Brazil and India ship rough marble for finishing to Italian standards. Sculptors around the world send small models to local artisans, who render them full-scale in marble. The traditions seem bound to continue, for enough marble to last another millennium lies in the hills.

Around the Carrara quarries, snow white marble debris covers the slopes. The bends in the mountain roads are so sharp that trucks hauling the stone can negotiate them only by traveling in reverse gear on alternate zigs and zags.

Swallowed up in the vast mouth of a
marble tunnel, a bulldozer waits to
move blocks cut from a deep vein. Although the open pit provides much
of the quarries' stone, some fine depos-
its can be reached only by burrowing
into the mountain.

Balanced on scaffolding wedged into the sheer rock face high above the quarry floor, workmen cut plugs. The deep holes they leave will hold explosives to blast away the surface stone, exposing the top-quality marble. The surface fragments are left scattered over the mountain.

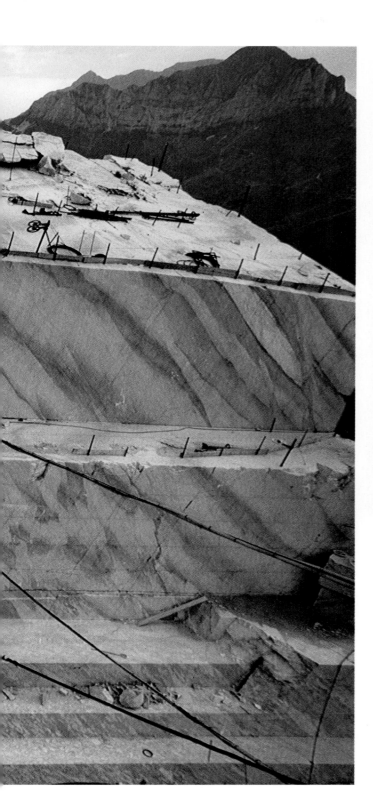

Severed from the mountainside with
the aid of hydraulic pulleys, a
huge marble block topples toward a
bed of rocky rubble, laid to cushion its
fall. The stone sometimes breaks
on impact, but the fragments are generally still large enough to use.

Rock-slicing cables festoon a stepped
quarry; the dark-veined marble is unusual in an area famous for its white
stone. Pulleys work the cables against
an abrasive mixture of sand and water
that gradually carves the mountain's
jagged profile into neat blocks.

Wearing the paper hat traditionally used by Carrara's stone workers to keep dust and debris out of their hair, an artisan of nearby Pietrasanta models a copy of the celebrated Greek sculpture of Laocoon and his sons. The studio is crowded with reproductions destined to adorn public buildings.

A craftsman roughs out a piece of modern sculpture with an electric drill. He has the sculptor's small-scale plaster model in front of him; calipers will help him transfer its exact proportions to the final, marble version.

In Carrara's main square, young artists from around the world labor at entries for the town's annual sculpture contest. Competing by invitation, they have two weeks to finish their works, which later go on permanent display along the local coastline.

65

A rare snowfall blankets vineyards on a high plateau in central Sicily. Although droughts and flash floods challenge grape growers, the island is Italy's second most productive wine region — after Puglia. Sicily's grapes are used for fortified Marsala as well as for full-bodied table wines.

AN EXACTING LAND

Italy is a harsh land, for all its beauty, and in the days when the land itself was the people's only resource, few of them ever managed an easy living from it. Although the broad valley of the Po River, stretching across northern Italy, contains some of the most productive agricultural land in Europe, four fifths of the country's familiar form — that ragged boot, swinging down from its icy Alpine thigh to aim a never-quite-delivered kick at arid and unruly Sicily — is made up of mountains and hills. Those that do not defy farmers altogether still tend to be too precipitous for machine cultivation. Erosion has stripped away much of the arable soil, especially in the south. Generations of grazing goats are partly to blame, but since Roman times humans have been equally responsible for the wasting of a once fertile landscape by burning trees to clear land and chopping them down for fuel and timber.

The climate, too, makes life difficult. For most outsiders, "sunny" is the adjective that leaps to join itself to "Italy," and the tourist brochures do not lie: Italy in summer has sun to spare, enough to shrivel crops where water is scarce. The winters, though, are cold, even in the south, where high inland plateaus make a mockery of ideas of a balmy Mediterranean climate. In the north, winter brings fog. Spring can swell rivers to destructive torrents, and autumn is often parched enough to frighten farmers. "We have four seasons here," Italians say cynically: "too dry, too cold, too wet and too hot."

Climate and topography are not the only hardships that Italy imposes on its people. Sometimes the very earth beneath their feet assails them. Although in terms of human history Italy can claim immense antiquity, it is a young country geographically: As mountains go, the Alps and Apennines are restive adolescents, and Italy sits squarely on Europe's most active seismic belt. Small earth tremors are almost a daily occurrence, and major earthquakes inflict devastation at depressingly frequent intervals. The Friuli region in the northeast, for example, was severely damaged in 1976; thousands died in the villages around Naples after an upheaval in 1980; and in 1984 scores of historic little towns in Umbria and Abruzzi, near Italy's geographic center, were badly hit.

Italy's lively geology also includes the only active volcanoes in continental Europe: Stromboli in the Tyrrhenian Sea, Etna in Sicily and Vesuvius near Naples. An eruption of Vesuvius in 79 A.D. destroyed the towns of Pompeii and Herculaneum; nowadays Vesuvius seems almost quiescent, but it has erupted more than once this century.

Pressure of numbers has long added to the strains on the nation. In the mid-19th century, the population was about 20 million; it had risen to about 30 million by 1900. With not enough good agricultural land to go around and virtu-

3

ally no industry to provide employment, Italians had little choice but to emigrate on a massive scale. The early emigrants chose Germany, France and Switzerland, but by the end of the 19th century, Italians were pouring into North and South America at a rate of hundreds of thousands a year. Emigration peaked in 1913, then fell during the interwar era to almost nothing as New World countries imposed quotas. In the two decades after World War II, the movement from Italy increased again: Approximately 300,000 Italians emigrated to Australia, and more than three million left for other European countries during the same period. Judging the effect of the exodus is difficult, for while many Italians have settled in their new homes for good, a substantial proportion will stay there only temporarily. People may leave Italy for a season, for a few years, even for a working lifetime, only to return to enjoy their hard-earned cash.

Partly because of the exiles' return, emigration has not succeeded in keeping a lid on the Italian population, which now stands at 57 million. The population density is only average — higher than in France and the United States, lower than in Britain and West Germany — but when set against the scarcity of cultivable or habitable land, it looks high indeed.

Italy's formidable terrain, where it has not actually driven its natives away altogether, has encouraged their segmentation into small, self-contained communities. Mountains do not make for easy communications, and poor communications tend to breed separatism. Local independence was strongest in medieval times, when most of the Italian communes were essentially self-governing. Starting in the 15th century, European power politics divided Italy between rival rulers until the country was unified in 1861.

Even today, more than a century after unification, Italians themselves frequently claim that there is no such thing as an Italian: only Lombards and Tuscans, Romans and Apulians, Venetians and Sicilians. They exaggerate. An excellent road network now provides a physical linkage unthinkable even 50 years ago, and television has gone a long way toward standardizing language, attitudes, consumer tastes and dress. Less subtly, the massive internal migrations of the postwar years stirred up the population, juxtaposing families with very different traditions and forcing them to find ways of living together comfortably as neighbors.

But regional loyalties are still very strong, a fact that was recognized in the 1947 republican constitution, which named 19 regions (since increased to 20 by the splitting of Abruzzi-Molise into its two constituent parts) to which certain government functions were to be devolved. Out of the 19 regions, Val d'Aosta, Trentino-Alto Adige, Friuli-Venezia Giulia, Sardinia and Sicily were granted special status and by the 1960s had a fair degree of autonomy. In these three frontier zones and two islands, suspicion of central government was especially strong, and threats to secede had made a radical move imperative. The remaining regions, however, had to wait until 1970 before they were allowed to elect assemblies empowered to legislate on planning and other regional matters.

Devolved government has under-scored local pride, but even without it regional attachments would have remained very strong. Regional identity exists first and foremost in people's minds; and it finds expression in the infinite gradation of dialect, custom and even cooking that Italy displays.

The differences between dialects were once a real barrier to communication, and they remain striking. The language now known as Italian is essentially the dialect of Tuscany (although the Tuscan accent is not the same as that of standard Italian). Tuscan is only one of many descendants of the old Latin tongue of the peninsula, but it was the one used by the poet Dante in his 14th-century masterpiece, the *Divina Commedia*. Subsequent Italian writers were deeply influenced by Dante's example, and Tuscan gradually came to be the language of the intelligentsia. It made virtually no headway as a language for ordinary people, however. At the time of Italian unification, it was spoken as a mother tongue by less than 3 percent of the population. Speakers of different dialects could barely comprehend each other. Thus the word *bianco* — "white" in standard Italian — becomes *biank* in parts of Piedmont, *giancu* in Liguria, *iango* in Campania, *aspro* in southern Calabria and *iancu* in Sicily.

Italian became the language of the new, unified state, and therefore the language of compulsory schooling — and of social advancement. Dialects were actively discouraged and regional writers, like everyone else, had to make the best of it. Ignazio Silone, the great novelist of Abruzzi, summed up the difficulties and resentments of many when he wrote in 1930 that "the Italian language is for us a foreign language, a dead language, a language whose vocabulary and grammar have no connection with our way of acting, our way of thinking, our way of expressing ourselves." He and others had learned to use it, of course, but "in the same way that we put on shoes and collar and tie for a visit to the city. Anyone can see our awkwardness."

Even today, Italian is far from being a universal tongue. According to a survey carried out in 1982, only 29 percent of the people use it at home. The rest of them speak either their traditional dialect or a mixture of that and the newly learned language.

Social customs, too, vary. Southerners still are more likely to enjoy a long after-lunch nap, for instance, while many northerners work through the afternoon. As far up the boot as Tuscany, the streets are alive on warm nights with families taking the air after dinner; but farther north, social life takes place indoors after dark. Italians are conservative about such habits, and "mixed" marriages — that is, those between spouses of different regions — often require a long period of delicate adjustment to new ways.

Adaptation comes hardest, perhaps, in the field of cookery, for food inspires the fiercest regional loyalties. Italian cooking is deservedly world-famous; but if you want to find an Italian restaurant, you must seek it out in Britain or in Germany, France or the United States, not in Italy, where local tastes and preferences are strong enough to overwhelm anything that might call itself a national cuisine.

True, pasta in one form or another appears on almost every table; but it arrives in an amazing profusion of shapes, many of which are firmly associated with a particular region and are dismissed as foreign nonsense in the

3

other regions. And if the pasta is boiled long enough to satisfy a Milanese, say, then anyone south of Rome will reject it as useless mush.

The risotto beloved of the *Milanesi* is virtually unknown in the south; the cornmeal concoction called polenta, much favored in the northeast, is eyed elsewhere with suspicious distaste; the pungent sauces that are so beloved in the south are considered barbaric in Florence; and so on *ad infinitum*. The proper way to cook things is the way that grandma cooked them; and grandma thought the same. But Italians are gradually getting used to fast food, and in this regard, regional differences are waning.

The country's diversity is an endless source of delight to the traveler; it makes a tour of Italy seem rather like a journey through a patchwork of little countries, each proudly distinct from its neighbors. Every one of the 20 regions has its own character; they do, however, fall into three broad geographical groupings: the north, the center and the south.

The north — "European" as opposed to "peninsular" Italy — covers roughly the area between the Alps and the Apennines; it has a history of enterprise and reasonably well-organized government. Its natives see themselves, with some justice, as more purposeful, more ambitious than other Italians. They are certainly richer. In appearance, they are mostly as dark-haired as the rest of the country's inhabitants, but they tend to be taller than the national average; and blue eyes and even blond hair are not startling rarities.

The center, which encompasses five regions and runs more or less from the northern edge of the Apennines to the vicinity of Rome, is not enormously dif-

On the Ligurian coast, a Mediterranean palette of ocher and umber colors many of the tall, narrow houses along La Spezia's waterfront. The town's deep natural harbor makes it an important base for the Italian Navy.

ferent; the distinction is more a matter of geographical convenience than it is a cultural divide. Much of the region spent centuries under the benevolent neglect of papal rule, and its economic advancement suffered correspondingly; but the area was also the birthplace of the Renaissance, and its inhabitants still like to think of themselves as intellectually superior to all others.

The south is another matter: not so much a geographical description as the statement of a problem that has lurked in the background of Italian politics ever since unification. Historically, the south is the part of Italy that once owed allegiance to the kings of Naples. Economically, it includes the most backward and depressed parts of Italy. Politically, it has come to imply — in the eyes of northerners, at least — a deep-seated distrust of authority combined with an incorrigible habit of corruption that defies all attempts at remediation. The south, in short, is different. Even its people — smaller and darker than elsewhere, sometimes almost Arab in appearance — seem a different race.

Italy stretches not much more than 600 miles from top to toe, but the cultural span is many times that.

A logical place to begin a tour of the country is Piedmont; for, despite its peripheral position in Italy's northwestern corner, it rightly claims to be the political kernel from which the modern nation grew. Italian unification was brought about in the 1850s and 1860s under Piedmont's royal house; for a brief period, Turin was the capital of the new state. In the 20th century, the Fiat factories have made Turin a capital of a different sort, the home of Italy's automobile industry.

Turin stands a little north of the area that produces what are arguably Italy's best wines. The hills around the town of Alba are the heartland of the Nebbiolo, reckoned by wine lovers to be Italy's noblest grape variety. The name is a reminder of the north's notorious winter fogs — *nebbie* — but there is nothing foggy about the region's powerful and long-matured wines, notably Barolo and Barbaresco. Many of the vineyards here are still using production methods that have scarcely changed in centuries, at least for their most serious — and most expensive — wines; others have welcomed the modern, more scientific techniques that were pioneered largely in California. Outsiders are unlikely to be able to contribute to the simmering controversy between traditionalists and modernists, since the best Barolos, no matter how they are made, rarely leave Piedmont.

Perhaps it is a pity when they do, for they taste best when accompanying good Piedmontese food: vegetables in a pungent sauce called *bagna cauda*, fine hams and salami, game and, most celebrated of all, the fragrant white truffles from the same hills of Alba that yield

In Milan, pedestrians cross the mosaic floors of the Galleria Vittoria Emanuele, Italy's largest shopping arcade and one of the city's favorite meeting places. Its architect, Giuseppe Mengoni, died in a fall from the glass roof days before the opening in 1878.

70

the finest Barolo. The Piedmontese are sometimes called "the Prussians of Italy": stern, hard-working and disciplined to a fault. But they are not too stern to enjoy a good meal.

Piedmont is not all high; indeed, its name means "at the foot of the mountain." In the Po valley, just west of Turin, graceful lines of poplars separate flourishing wheat fields and orchards, as well as the rice paddies — startlingly un-European in appearance — that furnish two thirds of Italy's rice supply.

The Po valley extends east into the next region — Lombardy, named after the Germanic tribes that colonized it in the Dark Ages. On the northern edge of the plain, Lakes Garda, Maggiore and Como provide Europe with some of its most glorious scenery. Gentle hills with lush vegetation flank parts of the lakes, wild cliffs mark other zones; the soaring Alps are a stunning backdrop.

With almost nine million people, Lombardy is Italy's most populous region; it is also the most productive, accounting for fully a third of Italian exports. Its agriculture is similar to Piedmont's, and the Lombards have long made ingenious use of the mighty Po. Since medieval times, a complex system of communally maintained canals has distributed irrigation water and provided protection against the river's regular floods. Leonardo da Vinci made plans for the system's improvement during his spell in the employ of the French ruler of Milan in the early part of the 16th century.

Milan, the capital of Lombardy, houses other products of Leonardo's protean genius, notably his recently restored *Last Supper* in the convent of Santa Maria delle Grazie. But Milan is better known as the hub of Italy's economic, financial and industrial activity than as a center of fine art. The city is a brusque and businesslike place, where dazzling high-rise office buildings jostle for space along elegant 19th-century boulevards and cramped medieval lanes. Along with the stylishness that has made it a capital of the design world, the city exudes a hard-headed

3

self-confidence that has been a Lombard hallmark for centuries.

Italy's second-largest city is unchallenged — at least within earshot of the Milanese, who have little time for the chaotic bureaucracy of Rome — as the "work capital" of the country. Business executives and managers point with pride at the number of international companies that have chosen Milan rather than Rome for their headquarters. Anti-Roman feeling is not confined to the managerial classes. In 1984, for example, the English soccer team from Liverpool beat Rome's team in a European Cup Final; most Italians took the defeat as a minor national calamity, but delighted Milanese graffiti artists blazoned "Thanks, Liverpool" on empty walls.

While Milan strives for success and recognition, Venice, the capital of the Veneto region, is content to bask in former glories. Once the headquarters of a maritime empire, the trade center where the West met the Orient, Venice began to lose its preeminence in the 16th century, when other nations successfully competed for a share in the trade with the East. Since then, the city has been little more than a glorious museum. Scarcely a modern building jars the eye amid the wonderful jumble of medieval, Renaissance and baroque architecture, and not a car is to be seen. Venice is built on an archipelago of islets in the center of a salt-water lagoon, and the only form of transport other than legs are the boats that ply the city's winding canals.

With its countless bridges dappled with reflections from the water, its brilliant churches with their bell towers leaning this way and that, its asymmetrical squares from which mysterious

72

Sheep graze below an avenue of Tuscan cypresses. In the 1970s, a fungus killed a quarter of the trees. Scientists saved the rest, preserving the landscape of the region, whose contours the cypresses have defined for centuries.

alleys lead off in all directions, Venice is to many the most entrancing of cities. Others are depressed by its crumbling stone and peeling façades and by the artificiality of Venice's modern existence. House prices and rents are understandably high. Many of Venice's fine old palaces are owned by foreigners and rich Milanese, while the ordinary people employed in Venice's tourist industry are often obliged to live in the unlovely mainland suburb of Mestre and then commute in along the causeway each day.

In the Veneto region, which forms the bulk of the old Venetian republic on the Italian mainland, almost every small town still boasts a statue of the lion of Saint Mark, emblem of the republic's former might. Now that Venice's real power has vanished, Veneto's biggest inland cities, Verona and Vicenza, have discovered a new economic center of gravity in Milan.

Vicenza was the birthplace of the colossally influential 16th-century architect Andrea Palladio. His pedimented, porticoed villas, elegant and harmonious in their proportions, remain among the most admired features of Veneto's flat, misty landscape, where truck farmers grow corn for the polenta that was once their staple diet. Their hold on the land is often tenuous: Floods are frequent, especially in the Po delta, where land-reclamation plans struggle to maintain an unstable dominance over the encroaching sea.

In Liguria, the last of the northern regions, lies the port that was once Venice's great maritime rival — Genoa. Unlike Venice, Genoa never lost its sea legs. It is Italy's biggest port and home of most of the shipbuilding industry — as well as of a people reputed, like the

3

Scots, to be shrewd and tightfisted.

The region is not large, a narrow crescent curving around the Mediterranean from the French border to Tuscany. The coast is Italy's Riviera, and its year-round gentle climate has encouraged predictable overdevelopment. Inland lie the Ligurian Apennines, the scene of fierce partisan fighting in World War II but now almost deserted. Over the last 30 years this region's inhabitants have given up subsistence hill farming for an easier city life.

Between the mountains and the sea, a whole series of steep valleys descends at right angles to the coast. Intensively terraced since Roman times, they now sparkle with greenhouses producing vast quantities of the fresh-cut flowers that are Liguria's most lucrative export. The narrow Ligurian valleys also yield some of Italy's most highly rated olive oil. There is a growing steel industry

along the coast from Genoa and Savona, and the coastal *autostrada* is an increasingly important route. Cutting across the rugged Ligurian topography, it winds through a breathtaking succession of tunnels and viaducts that make an impressive advertisement for modern Italian engineering.

The Apennines continue southward into Emilia-Romagna, the most northerly of the central regions, which extends as far as the Po. About half of its area is mountainous, but most of its principal cities as well as some of the best agricultural land in Italy lie in the fertile Emilian plain. Once it was part of the Papal States, administered directly by the Catholic Church. Now it has a well-earned reputation for anticlericalism, as well as for radical politics. The political attitude is partly a reaction against the region's landlords, whose large and technically advanced farms

for decades employed landless laborers at subsistence wages.

Today, much of Emilia-Romagna exudes prosperity; Bologna, its capital, is aptly called "La Grassa" — "The Fat." Bologna is generally agreed to be the gastronomic capital of Italy. Its specialities are not particularly sophisticated, simply very good: innumerable kinds of fresh pasta, sometimes flavored with spinach and perhaps stuffed with meat and vegetables or ricotta cheese, almost always served with plenty of excellent cream; huge plates of boiled meats; and of course the world-famous ham and cheese of nearby Parma.

Beyond Emilia-Romagna, the spine of the Apennines curves toward the Adriatic side of the peninsula. Tuscany lies to the west, between the ridgeline of the mountains and the Mediterranean Sea. The region is mostly hill country, with a fair share of mountains, and the rolling, richly wooded landscape gives the impression of being gentler than it actually is.

It is first-class wine country, the home of Chianti. Italy's best-known wine is made to a high standard of quality, not least because the average Tuscan producer is an enthusiastic convert to the new, scientific oenology. Dingy cellars filled with deteriorating 19th-century equipment have become rare; instead there are gleaming stainless steel and judiciously applied modern biochemistry. Rivers of Chianti inundate the world, but Tuscany's less abundant wines — including Vino Nobile de Montepulciano and the highly regarded Brunello di Montalcine — are little known abroad, and in fact, they rarely travel farther than Florence.

Florence, Tuscany's capital, was the main crucible of Renaissance painting; it remains a great cultural center and an irresistible magnet for lovers of fine art. Although it has acquired an expanding suburbia with a belt of light industry, the old city center is much as it was in the 15th century, when its ruling Medici family was at the height of its power. Florence's people, too, have changed little: It can be an unsettling experience to walk out of the city's great Uffizi Gallery and see on the streets outside the same kind of faces that Botticelli or da Vinci painted 500 years ago.

Tuscans are something of a race apart. At once imaginative and dour, hard-working and mischievous, they have a reputation for tough bargaining and a certain perverse cunning. According to the Tuscan writer Curzio Malaparte, "When others weep, we laugh, and when others laugh, we stand and watch them laughing, without batting an eyelid, in silence — until the smile freezes on their lips."

South of Tuscany is Umbria — Italy's green heart, as the area's own publicity justifiably calls it, and the only region that includes neither a seacoast nor an international border. Umbria is predominantly agricultural, and its farming practices are relatively traditional; the mountainous terrain allows only limited scope for the mechanization now typical in the Po valley.

Umbria's greatest asset is the appeal to visitors of its beautiful landscape and the exquisite old towns that cap every likely hill. Perugia, the region's capital, is an almost perfect medieval hill town, naturally compact and preserved as much by civic pride as by Umbria's rigorous planning laws. Orvieto, Gubbio and Spoleto are equally lovely; and Assisi has been a major tourist attraction ever since its beloved Saint Francis died in the 13th century. The town has survived 700 years of pilgrims and sight-seers with an aplomb that few modern resorts can match.

The Adriatic coast of northern Italy is itself an unfortunate example of unrestricted tourist development: concrete, concrete and more concrete, in an almost unbroken line from Rimini and Cattolica in Emilia-Romagna through Ancona, the regional capital of The Marches, to the mouth of the River Tronto at The Marches' southernmost extremity. This area was the border province that divided the corrupt and torpid Papal States to the north from the corrupt and torpid Kingdom of the Two Sicilies to the south; today, the region shares with the south a serious problem of rural depopulation.

But the mountainous interior is not all abandoned farms. Notoriously bad roads — modernized now, but still long and twisting — have protected fine old towns such as Urbino and Loreto from

A herd of oxen fording a stream *(above)* and their dashing *buttero*, or cowboy *(above, left)*, reflect the economy of the Maremma, north of Rome on the west coast. A vast reclamation project drained its malarial marshes, leaving fertile farmland and pasture for sturdy local breeds of horses and cattle.

3

The medieval bell tower of San Donato crowns the steep cliffs of Civita, near Lake Bolsena. Called the Crumbling City because of its erosion problems, the town was once linked to the larger town of Bagnoregio nearby. Today, Civita is reached by a viaduct *(center)* across a half-mile-wide gulch.

the worst ravages of tourism. The deep valleys and rugged mountain slopes that so impede communication at least give The Marches some of the most impressive scenery in Italy, with spectacular waterfalls and grottoes. It is the kind of landscape that encourages independence, and on the edge of The Marches is a quaint historical anomaly that still defies the process of Italian unification: the miniature independent republic of San Marino, whose 24 square miles support a population of around 20,000, a government and even a minuscule standing army.

Real government, of course, is the business of Rome, across the Apennines in the region of Latium — though Rome, too, has its comic-opera aspects. As journalist Peter Nichols wrote perceptively: "To the south, it personifies the heartless concentration of power which the southerner regards as constantly working against his due interests; to the north, it is an intolerable burden which is holding back the development of enterprise and modern society, like some elderly, overdressed, self-centered old mistress who refuses to give way to the new young wife." But provincials have complained about Rome for more than 2,000 years, and Rome has usually managed to fascinate and seduce its critics: The Eternal City did not get its name for nothing.

After the glorious days of the Roman Republic and Empire, the invasions of Vandals, Goths and other barbarians temporarily put Rome out of business. But before long, it found a new lease on life as headquarters of the Catholic Church. It did not become part of modern, united Italy until 1870, nine years after the rest of the country had come together, but it was then the inevitable choice as capital. The city saw a tremendous surge in public building in the late 19th century as each ministry vied with every other to provide itself with headquarters accommodation for its essential bureaucrats — a process that has continued to the present day.

But Rome remains above all a city of the 17th century — the heyday of papal splendor, when baroque sculptors adorned every skyline with gesticulating saints. English travel writer H. V. Morton remarked, "The Rome that first prints itself upon the eye and the mind is not classical Rome, buried beneath the streets and covered with its shroud of Time, or medieval Rome, which now consists mainly of a stray and lovely campanile, or 19th-century gigantism, or modern Rome, a mostly hideous mass of concrete, but this gay, declamatory Rome of the Popes, with its peachy, golden palaces, its once quiet piazze, its glorious fountains and its look of just having happened on some happy and fortunate day."

Officially, the Catholic Church no longer rules the city — only the tiny statelet of the Vatican, where about a thousand permanent residents and 3,500 outside workers administer its worldwide congregation and attend to the floods of visitors who assail it every day. Some come as pilgrims, others as tourists eager to gaze at the famous frescoes by Michelangelo and Raphael.

With its two bureaucracies and its massive tourist industry, Rome appears to have an insatiable appetite for people. From a peak population of around a million in classical times, it shrank to well under 30,000 in the Middle Ages. But now it is Italy's largest city, with close to three million residents. It lures them from Latium and elsewhere and rapidly turns them into authentic *Romani,* wry and street-wise.

3

To the east and south of Rome, Italy's real problems begin. This is the zone of hardship, from which millions have fled in search of a better life either in the cities or abroad.

As the crow flies, the mountainous Abruzzi region, on a latitude with Latium, is not far from Rome; but until an *autostrada* link was built in 1970, the journey on the ground was a long one, across the highest point in the whole Apennine chain. The isolation of the Abruzzi people no doubt helped them acquire their unmerited reputation as the comic dimwits of Italy.

Traditionally, sheep raising provided a scanty living here, as in neighboring Molise. Now, however, a winter sports industry is being built up, and the Abruzzi National Park attracts patient nature watchers hoping to catch a glimpse of its rarest and most renowned denizens, the brown bear and the Apennine wolf.

Campania, south of Latium, provides a startling contrast to the windswept mountains of Abruzzi and Molise. In the summer, driving toward Naples from Rome is like driving into a furnace. Tree-clad hills give way to scrub slopes and bare earth, cactus begins to proliferate by the roadside, and the soil itself changes from a European brown to a tropical red.

But where there is water, the soil is fertile enough. The Campanian plain is a gigantic kitchen garden, producing peas and beans, peppers, tomatoes, eggplants and assorted fruits in its volcanically enriched earth. It is also the home of the principal consumers of this wealth of produce: the residents of the astonishing city of Naples.

Naples is teeming. Most of its population of well over a million can aspire at best to a cramped little apartment, and

Roman traffic crawls along the Via della Conciliazione in front of St. Peter's Basilica. To create such broad vistas and the triumphal parade routes that are a feature of modern Rome, Mussolini demolished much of the medieval city in the 1930s.

many of them are condemned to the worst slum housing in Europe. In compensation, they live most of their lives on the streets. The city is full of cars, from purring Mercedes to battered old Fiat 500s, coexisting with the people in a peculiarly Neapolitan way. "You have to stop at the green lights here," warned a driver; "in Naples, you can be sure that someone will be going through the red." It hardly needs saying that Naples is also full of noise. Despite the factories and refineries that disfigure the once-glorious Bay of Naples, there is by no means enough work for the city's inhabitants. Many can only hope to live by the celebrated Neapolitan art of "getting by": an odd hour's labor here, an afternoon as an unlicensed taxi driver there, a little wheeling and dealing somewhere else, and perhaps, if no one is looking, a lucky find — a carelessly chained bicycle, say, or a tourist's handbag. And there is contraband on a huge scale. At night, powerful launches bring smuggled cigarettes and other goods into the city's harbor. During the daytime, people sell them openly in the streets, ig-

nored by the police. To be sure, Contraband makes fortunes for a few gang leaders and a handful of corrupt politicians. More to the point, however, it provides a modest living for thousands of Neapolitans who would otherwise be destitute, desperate and dangerous. It is no wonder that the authorities choose to turn a blind eye: Naples lives on the edge of a volcano in more than one sense, and one day it could well be the city itself that erupts, instead of smoky old Vesuvius above it.

South of Naples is the beautiful Sorrento peninsula, with its steep cliffs rising from an azure sea, with its olive and citrus groves. Tourism has long sustained the inhabitants both here and on the island of Capri, which is less than three miles from the southern tip of the Sorrento peninsula.

The mountainous island is blessed with luxuriant vegetation and a limpid atmosphere. For a place of extraordinary tranquillity and beauty, Capri hides an unexpectedly sinister past. The Roman Emperor Tiberius was seduced by the charms of the place in 27 A.D.; until then, he had reigned wisely and beneficently, but the story of his 10-year sojourn on the island is not an edifying one. According to contemporary writers, he amused himself on Capri with every sort of cruel and obscene entertainment. He built a dozen great villas on the perimeter of Capri and incorporated into them dungeons, torture chambers and places of execution; in one villa that has been excavated, some of these macabre spots can be visited today.

Calabria, the narrow toe of the Italian boot, has Italy's most spectacular coastline, but voracious, unplanned development is blighting many parts of it that are not protected by sheer cliffs. In addition to hotels and vacation villas, there are dozens of ugly skeletons of half-completed houses. These are the work of Calabrian emigrants who return for a week or two each year, if money permits, and build a little more of the home they hope to retire to.

Calabria was once a Greek colony; the local dialect, guttural and impenetrable to outsiders, still owes as much to Greek as to Latin. And buried deep in the mountains, there are villages where Albanian is the native tongue. These communities date back to the 15th century, when the ancestors of the present inhabitants were refugees from the Turkish conquest of their land. Their successors have managed to retain their cultural identity for two reasons: physical isolation, of course, but also the fact that they are descended from the cream of the Albanian nation, people who had fought their conquerors bitterly and emigrated only when the last battles had been lost.

Basilicata, the instep of Italy, is the south at its cruelest. Stark, with hills as bare as slag heaps, the landscape looks like spoil from some monstrous excavation, and the grim little towns that are huddled together on the hilltops seem no more than the last of the earth's leavings. Rivers, for most of the year, are little more than gray beds of gravel, waiting to serve simply as run-off channels for the ferocious autumn rains, which never come to nourish the land, only to scour it mercilessly.

The countryside has few farmhouses. The people who remain — Basilicata's population has fallen steadily for 40 years — live in cramped towns that are little more than barracks for agricultural laborers. Each morning before dawn, men and women alike set

A woman takes down washing outside her *trullo*, a whitewashed stone dwelling of ancient design found only in Apulia, Italy's "heel." Perfectly suited to a hot climate, the thick walls of the building keep its interior cool, while the conical roof channels precious rain water to a cistern.

3

off together to walk great distances to their fields; each evening, after dusk, they return home.

In her book *Women of the Shadows*, the American Ann Cornelisen writes:

To go to the fields is almost a reflex, conditioned by the absolute lack of any other work. You go, even when you might not have to. The donkey needs fodder: you cut it by hand, sometimes just along the verges, and shove it into the sacks that hang from the saddle. While you're about it, you pull up wild greens for a salad — a little sorrel, dandelions, whatever there is. You weed your patch of wheat, you loosen the dirt around the beans, tie up a vine. You look over to see how your neighbor's crops are coming. Not really that you hoped yesterday's hailstorm had beaten them down, but there would be some justice if . . . . You collect a few twigs for kindling. And finally at some invisible cue of light not changed but about to change, the long walk back to town. Five miles, ten — a long way with nothing to think about except how to get a bit more land, a job — how to feed your children. Your children. Will they live like this? You don't ride the donkey; he needs his strength too. The click of his hooves, the scrape of your boots and you almost fall asleep walking.

Whenever the weather permits, the people spend their leisure time in the streets — many of which are unpaved and lined with open sewers. The men sit there gossiping, surveying the outside world, while the women turn their backs to it and knit, compelled by custom to dress in black and face the crumbling walls of their houses.

Even in Basilicata, however, the picture is not one of unrelieved wretchedness. In the town of Matera, for instance, most of the population used to live, livestock and all, in the *sassi* — a honeycomb of little caves. Now the *sassi* are almost empty, and a bright new town has sprung into life above and around them. Some of the new prosperity is based on money sent home by emigrants working in the north, but government investment is responsible for launching a few local industries, too. Matera's stores are well stocked and always have plenty of customers.

Of the three southernmost regions, only Apulia — the heel of Italy — has managed to achieve anything like real economic success. Its natural advantages are considerable: more than half of its area is flat and, despite a chronic water shortage, much of the land is as fertile as any other region in Italy. Vines, fruit and olive trees as bulky as small oaks have been growing in Apulia for centuries; industry, too, has a relatively long history. Taranto has been a strategic naval base for Italy since the Suez Canal opened in 1869; with Brindisi and the regional capital of Bari, it forms part of an industrial triangle that is strong in petrochemicals and steel.

The five so-called special regions of Italy owe their greater autonomy — and the earlier date of their receiving it — to special problems. The three northern units — Val d'Aosta, Trentino-Alto Adige and Friuli-Venezia Giulia — are all frontier regions, each with its own history of dissenting minorities; the islands of Sicily and Sardinia came out of World War II seething with secessionist resentment because of their years of neglect at the hands of the central administration.

Val d'Aosta is the smallest of all the regions, an enclave in the high Alps around Mont Blanc. French used to be the inhabitants' principal language. The growth of a winter-sports industry has largely halted a troublesome decline in its population; local autonomy — and a reasonable level of material well-being — have greatly weakened its still-active separatist movement.

Trentino-Alto Adige's situation is more complex. The German-speaking province of Alto Adige (otherwise known as the South Tyrol) was Italy's main reward for victory over Austria in World War I. Many of its inhabitants were less than enthusiastic about the transfer of sovereignty, especially when Mussolini's Fascist government directed a stream of immigrants into the province in order to inflate the Italian-speaking minority. Mussolini also banned German speakers from public office and refused to permit German surnames to be used.

Unsurprisingly, then, the leaders of the postwar Italian Republic had some very unhappy and suspicious people to deal with. In the end, a hybrid region was created that included the Italian-speaking area of Trentino. Alto Adige and Trentino, as well as the region as a whole, were each allowed to control their own administration.

But the creation of a region with an overall Italian majority did nothing to mollify the German speakers in Alto Adige. In the 1960s, they turned to violence and succeeded in gaining more power for themselves and more protection for their language. Since then, the region has settled down, the old conflicts still simmering but masked by the general prosperity of both its parts.

That other composite region, Friuli-Venezia Giulia, grew out of the need to provide a hinterland for the ailing port of Trieste, which almost became part of Yugoslavia at the end of World War II. Trieste is a beautiful, haunted city; its *raison d'être* vanished with the Austro-

Lines of laundry garland a narrow street in Naples, the most densely populated city in Europe. In recent years, local authorities have built much housing on the periphery of the city, but some 100,000 Neapolitans still live in one-room dwellings in the center.

3

Hungarian Empire, for which it was once the major outlet. Italians have, however, always been deeply attached to the place.

The region is a highly artificial creation. Venezia Giulia is all that remains of a much larger province, which once included the peninsula of Istria, successfully claimed by Yugoslavia in the postwar settlement; the agricultural territory known as Friuli has traditional links with Venice rather than with Trieste. The area's economy was somewhat moribund even before the 1976 earthquake, which devastated several villages and badly damaged the historic city of Udine.

Sicily, at least, is not artificial; indeed no one could possibly have invented this island. The largest island in the Mediterranean, it is also the largest of all the Italian regions, and with approximately five million people, it is

one of the more populous. It does possess some advantages: very fertile land, though rainfall is often insufficient; and mineral reserves that are plentiful, at least by Italian standards. But Sicily's regional government has been an unmitigated disaster, afflicted by chronic corruption and *clientelismo* — the habit of distributing jobs and contracts as political patronage.

The island — at any rate, its western half and the regional capital, Palermo — is also the home of the Mafia. Clearly, the clammy hand of criminal conspiracy is largely responsible for the poor state of local industry and the high level of emigration.

Yet Sicily has made an immense contribution to Italian culture — especially, in modern times at least, to Italian literature. From Luigi Pirandello, the influential playwright who probed the boundary between reality and illusion,

to the Nobel prize-winning poet Salvatore Quasimodo, Sicily's writers have given their homeland a powerful voice.

Many of these writers have found their themes in the island's social distress: In the novel *Mastro-don Gesualdo*, for example, the 19th-century author Giovanni Verga set his obsessively ambitious hero against the bitter realities of his poverty-stricken island. More recently, the shrewd and observant novels of Leonardo Sciascia have managed to penetrate to the very heart of the present-day Mafia.

Sicily is also remarkable for the number of outstanding, honest politicians it has exported — as opposed to the less-than-upright examples who are still at home. Riccardo Lombardi, from Enna, in the center of the island, was a famous partisan during World War II and a key member of the Socialist party until his death in 1984. Somewhat to the left of his party's center, Lombardi involved himself fiercely and passionately in every issue, but he lacked the ruthless personal ambition that tempted many of his colleagues into corruption. Ugo La Malfa, a Palermo resident, was for many years the leader of the small Republican party. He shaped it into an organ that has earned universal respect for its thoughtful policies and high standards.

Italy's other great Mediterranean island, Sardinia, has also sent some of its best political minds to the mainland — most notably Enrico Berlinguer, who until his death in 1984 was the popular leader of the Italian Communist party. Generally, though, Sardinia has kept to itself, in an isolation that has been anything but splendid.

The island is a poor place even now, mountainous and lacking in good inland roads. Many of its inhabitants are

The brilliant blue waters of the Tyrrhenian Sea lap the sharply hewn coast of Lipari, the largest island in the Aeolian archipelago north of Sicily. The island's volcanic rock has provided profitable exports over the centuries: glasslike obsidian in ancient times and abrasive pumice stone today.

Mount Etna, whose name comes from the Greek for "I burn," smolders above Taormina, a Sicilian resort town. At a height of more than 10,700 feet, Etna is Europe's highest volcano. It has erupted on an average of more than once a decade; in 1928, its lava flow buried the nearby town of Mascali.

still shepherds, following their flocks in seminomadic fashion across the high pastures of the interior. Sardinia's sharp and well-matured sheep's-milk cheeses are renowned throughout Italy; and so are its bandits, with their tradition of robbery and kidnapping. Unlike Sicily's *mafiosi,* however, whose income and power derive from the wealth of an organized society, Sardinian bandits are the outward manifestation of a hard life, close to the margins of survival, embodying cruel but ancient traditions of honor and vendetta.

Still, a killer is a killer, whether dressed in a stylish gray suit or a rough sheepskin vest. No one is sorry that banditry on Sardinia is gradually dying out — least of all the growing number of people there who now depend on the tourist industry for their living. For the moment, kidnapping remains a lucrative business on the island; but in time, economic development may make banditry an obsolete occupation.

It is unlikely to make Sardinians any less dour and remote, but nobody is asking them to change their essential ways. Italians have realized that uniformity is unattainable, at least in the short term; regional feeling runs too deep. Rather than striving for standardization, they have made a virtue of diversity. They relish their local cooking, their dialect literature. They are at ease with their differences. □

RIGORS OF LIFE
IN THE FORSAKEN SOUTH

Want and endless toil have always been the lot of the rural poor throughout southern Italy, but hardship is at its most acute in Basilicata. The harsh life of the region was vividly portrayed in the book *Christ Stopped at Eboli,* written more than 40 years ago by Carlo Levi. The title is drawn from a local way of describing the godforsaken remoteness of the land south of Eboli.

Levi, an artist and doctor, was exiled to the south in 1935 for opposing Mussolini's invasion of Ethiopia. He was sent first to Grassano but later lived for almost a year in Aliano — Gagliano in his book. His medical training brought him into close contact with the villagers, who were plagued by malaria and the diseases of deprivation.

Since Levi's sojourn in Aliano, the hardship and isolation have been mitigated: People now own television sets, telephones and cars; the roads are paved, and there are more of them; irrigation systems have made the land more productive; state industries have created some new jobs. But prosperity continues to be elusive. Were Levi alive today he might still write of "this shadowy land," where "evil is not moral but is only the pain residing forever in earthly things."

Don Pietro Dilenge, Aliano's priest, banters with four women who have been picking tomatoes in fields near the village. The priest, faced with high unemployment among Aliano's youth, set up an agricultural cooperative in the late 1970s; it has had some success, despite the area's poor soil.

Below the village of Aliano, trees and scrub maintain a precarious hold on the unstable clay soil of the steep ravines. The villagers must contend not only with erosion and a scarcity of water for irrigation, but with earthquakes — one of which destroyed a third of Aliano's houses in 1980.

Caves at the base of a cliff near Aliano *(above)* serve as storage for tools and as shelter for newborn kids and their mothers. Other goats are penned at night beneath the rock face *(right)*. In Levi's day, many families lived almost entirely off these beasts, which need no pasture but browse on the area's thorny bushes. Today, the goats are still a mainstay of the village's economy: Their milk is sold to a cooperative and then to industry for cheese making.

In Grassano, an elderly man prepares a
meal in his one-room home. Houses
have changed since Levi wrote: "They
were all alike . . . one room almost
entirely filled by an enormous bed . . .
in it slept the whole family." Then, animals shared their owners' living
quarters; today, goats are kept outside.

On a Grassano street, the bright modern clothes of youth contrast sharply with the black mourning garb of an earlier generation. The older villagers, who grew up with constant hunger and deprivation, are noticeably shorter than the children of postwar years.

A woman waits outside a modernized house in a village near Grassano, while a mule stands under the archway. Most of the villagers farm scattered pieces of land in the steep hills nearby, where mules and donkeys often work more efficiently than machinery.

An old farm near Matera, the capital of
Basilicata, is dwarfed by a chemical
complex on its doorstep. This industrial plant is still in operation — unlike
many that were set up by the government in the postwar years in an attempt
to improve the economy of the south.

In the old part of Matera, stone façades
mask cave dwellings cut into the steep
hill. Now mostly deserted, in Levi's
time the caves were overcrowded, providing shelter for whole families as
well as their goats and pigs.

AN INSTINCT FOR DRAMA

The Italians have a genius for drama that manifests itself in both their arts and their everyday life. The people who invented opera and infused painting with a new power of expression during the Renaissance know instinctively how to maximize an artistic or emotional effect, how to enliven a scene with movement and energy. Italian speech, in all its melodiousness, is incomplete without the accompanying emphatic gestures and facial expressions that turn ordinary moments into a kind of theatrical performance.

An important facet of this gift for drama is summed up by the expression *bella figura*. It means style, making the best of yourself, conveying a pleasing impression of yourself to others. *Bella figura* is carefully cultivated and earned by hard work. Many Italians are blessed with good looks to begin with, and they take care to enhance their beauty by walking with pride, speaking with fluency and assurance and, if they can possibly afford to do so, dressing in the latest fashion, even if it means having to skimp on other personal comforts. Clothes are a vitally important medium for sending out a personal message to the world. Fashion dictates that everyone who can manage it appears in a new outfit at least twice a year, and that means finding one's own particular niche in the season's prescribed canon of color and shapes.

This penchant for dramatically costumed entrances and exits plays squarely into the hands of clothing designers, who have made Italy one of the homes of fashion ever since the end of World War II. While the panjandrums of Parisian haute couture were busy blowing up a fresh storm each year, the Rome of Galitzine, Valentino and Antonelli became the Eternal City of elegance, producing its collection with an aristocratic detachment and an unfailing eye for detail.

Florence is another of Italy's fashion centers — as befits the city whose Renaissance art patrons had built their fortunes on weaving and the cloth trade. But Milan is now undoubtedly Italy's fashion capital. Its many famous design houses — Missoni, Armani, Versace and Krizia are just four of the best — specialize in casual elegance. They are as famous for their ravishing fabrics as for the cut of their garments. Sumptuous leather outfits and stylish knitwear are among their fortes.

Deriving so much pleasure from the ever-changing tableau of fashion, Italians also love spectacular costumes, and they have ample opportunity to enjoy these. In Rome, objects of universal admiration are the pope's Swiss guards, whose uniform is a dazzling assemblage of yellow, red and blue, artfully arranged in individual ribbons of color. Not to be outdone, the president of the republic, in the Quirinal Palace, is guarded by a corps of extra-tall cavalrymen, resplendent in steel breastplates, plumed hats and huge sabers. The var-

As her gondola glides alongside moorings in the Venetian lagoon, a spectral reveler alights to join in the pre-Lent festivities of the annual Carnival. The eerie anonymity of the veil and mask gives her the freedom that thieves, gamblers and lovers have enjoyed for centuries during Carnival.

4

ious units of the army, navy and air force pride themselves on wearing a fantastic variety of dress uniforms harking back to earlier epochs of Italian history. The crack regiment of army sharpshooters, the *bersaglieri,* wear great bunches of iridescent feathers in their mountaineers' hats, while the *carabinieri,* or armed police, when on ceremonial duty, become the cynosure of all eyes in their Napoleonic-era finery, complete with crossed bandoleers and broad black hats.

In one way or another, nearly everybody has the opportunity to appear several times a year as an actor or extra in some local piece of street theater, be it a festival or a historical commemoration. During the first week in January, many of the communities sponsor "living pageants" of the arrival of the Magi for the Feast of the Three Kings. At Easter time there are countless Good Friday celebrations throughout Italy: Taranto, for example, is famous for its parade of hooded penitents and flagellants, who take 14 hours to make the rounds of the city. On Ascension Day at Cocullo, in the region of Abruzzi, local tradition calls for a serpent procession, in which pilgrims and singers carry live snakes in their hands, and the image of the patron saint, San Domenico, is ringed with vipers.

In July, the Venetians celebrate the end of the plague of 1576 by building a bridge of boats across the wide canal of the Giudecca to the Church of the Redemption, with nocturnal fireworks and concerts in the courtyard of the Doge's Palace. In September, the town of Arezzo stages mock jousting against dummy Saracens.

Three times a year — in May, September and December — the whole of

Naples turns out to bear witness to the Miracle of San Gennaro, the local patron saint whose dried blood, kept in two glass vials in a chapel of the cathedral, is supposed to liquefy for the occasion. If the miracle does not occur, disaster is said to be imminent for Naples — but rarely do the officiating clergy fail to announce that the transformation has indeed come about.

The most celebrated and spectacular of all these festivities is the annual Carnival, which is held during the period that precedes Lent. In recent years, Venice has recaptured its position as one of the world's favorite places for such merrymaking.

During the 18th century, the city boasted the longest and the most licentious of all the European carnivals, but in the more sober age that followed, the tradition was allowed to lapse. It was revived in the early 1980s, ostensibly for the benefit of the tourist industry, but more likely because the Venetians themselves wanted another opportunity to dress up and let off steam.

For 10 frenzied days, inhibitions are thrown to the winds as masked, costumed revelers crowd into the narrow alleys and windy piazzas of the city that was once the merchant capital of the eastern Mediterranean. At the height of the celebration, as many as 80,000 people fill the great square in front of St. Mark's Basilica.

In earlier centuries, however, Rome was the real headquarters of the Carnival, and many of the popes actively encouraged the custom. The Roman merrymaking involved pageants, races, banquets and theatrical performances as well as the traditional street festivities, with costumed crowds singing coarse ditties while pelting one another with sweetmeats. One of the highlights was a race of riderless Berber horses along the broad street known to this day as the Corso, meaning "racecourse." The horses were led in amid shouts and yells from the crowd; strips of tinsel were fastened to their backs and lead balls spiked with needles dangled from their sides, spurring them to a frenzy. A furious struggle ensued as the grooms tried to restrain the animals until, at a signal, the starter's rope fell to the ground and the horses charged pell-mell down the street. At the finish line, another set of grooms had the unenviable job of catching and controlling the maddened beasts.

When the German poet Goethe visited Rome in the 1780s, this astonishing spectacle struck him as the perfect symbol of the unbridled sensuality that reigned among the people at Carnival time. Because he was well read in the history of ancient Rome, he realized that the celebration he had just witnessed was simply a latter-day version of the equally licentious Saturnalia — the week-long festival in honor of the pagan god Saturn — when sexuality ran rampant, all distinctions of rank were set aside and everyone enjoyed a topsy-turvy freedom of expression. The Carnival was, therefore, one powerful instance, not only of the Italians' inborn sense of theater, but of their instinct for cultural continuity. Perhaps no other people in Europe have a more intimate relationship with their distant past.

While carnivals and pageants bring history to life in the streets of Italy, time-honored dramatic forms flourish on its stages. The works of a few playwrights from the past, such as the 18th-century Venetian writer of comedies, Carlo Goldoni, are still performed today. However, the most pervasive legacies from other eras are musical drama — that is, opera — and traditional theatrical modes that depend on actors improvising around classical plots and stock characters.

One version of extempore drama that survives today is the puppet theater of Sicily — a thriving tradition that has hardly changed for centuries. The brilliantly painted marionettes stand about 30 inches tall and weigh up to 45 pounds, so that they have to be maneuvered by strong handlers working iron rods as well as strings. The voices are supplied by puppeteers whose families have usually been involved in the puppet theater for several generations.

Among their stock characters are puppet knights that are fully armed and capable of drawing their swords from their scabbards to fight the battles of chivalry — against serpents, villains, giants and Saracens on behalf of truth, justice and the honor of fair damsels. A favorite vehicle for such action is Ariosto's *Orlando Furioso,* the great 16th-century adaptation of the legend of the knight Roland doing battle with the enemies of Christendom. An even more kinetic drama enacts the wholesale slaughter of French invaders by native Sicilians in 1281; the so-called Sicilian Vespers is one instance of the struggle against outside oppressors that has always been the central theme of the island's history. Strong men have been known to weep real tears because these performances evoke the passions and fantasies of their thirst for justice and vengeance.

The puppets' fast physical and verbal footwork is paralleled in another Italian tradition, that of the *commedia dell'arte,* which first made its appearance in about 1530. It was a frothy, exciting kind of theater; unlike the amateur

theatricals popular at the Renaissance courts, the *commedia* required arts and skills that only professionals could muster: not only acting, singing, dancing and fencing, but also such sidelines as juggling, conjuring and acrobatics. Handstands and cartwheels were an integral part of the action.

The plays were improvised around stock situations — a rich man is bested by his cunning valet, who also makes off with the beautiful woman, for example — but the plots were of secondary importance. What mattered was the speed, surprise and comedy generated by the cast — a minimum of eight recurring characters who among them represented a spectrum of human, all too human, foibles and follies.

There was Zanni the comic servant, clever, greedy and shameless, and always in revolt against oppression and injustice. One variation on the Zanni character was the wily Arlecchino (Harlequin), portrayed as a valet who car-

ried a rabbit's tail as the emblem of his courage and wore a patched-up coat of many colors; a second was the crooknosed, ill-mannered Pulcinella, later to beget the English Mr. Punch. Other characters included Pantalone — a pompous, opinionated Venetian merchant — and a military captain known variously as Spavento, Giangurgolo, Il Vappo or Rogantino — a cowardly swaggerer, forever boasting of his past exploits. On the distaff side, there was Columbina, a pert and lovely creature in ravishing décolletage, who provided these outrageous farces with an element of love interest.

Theater historians searching for the origins of these characters found that their progenitors were much older than the Renaissance. In the Italian arts all roads lead back to ancient Rome: In this case, the starting point was the Atellan farce, a genre of sketches about country bumpkins and city slickers, including Maccus the fool, Manducus the

glutton, Pappus the ridiculous old man and Dossennus the wily rogue. Originating around the town of Atella in Campania, the form was taken up by the Romans in the third century B.C. and enjoyed for more than two centuries. The Romans added their own polish and even wrote down some of the scripts, but they always kept a rustic coarseness of language and incident.

The Atellan farce was eventually replaced by other kinds of comedy, but when it resurfaced centuries later as the *commedia dell'arte,* it made a profound impact on European theater. In the 1570s, as an insurance against homesickness, the great Italian heiress Catherine de Médicis, who had gone to Paris to marry the heir to the French throne, afterward Henry II, invited a *commedia* troupe to come to France to perform for her. Decades later, the French playwright Molière was enchanted by the actors, and he used some of their tricks and stock situations in his comedies.

Before long, the popularity of the *commedia dell'arte* spread to the rest of 16th-century Europe, notably Germany, Russia and England, all of which were visited by companies of Italian players. Today, there is no permanent *commedia* company in Italy, but the form lives on elsewhere: The world's oldest surviving *commedia*-style troupe performs in the Copenhagen amusement park known as the Tivoli Gardens.

The *commedia* characters have contributed enormously to other forms of theater, and none more than the madcap Zanni. Both circus acts and slapstick comedy depend on borrowings from his repertoire. The world-famous comics of movies and television in the 20th century — Charlie Chaplin, the Marx Brothers, the Keystone Cops and Monty Python — can trace their genealogy directly back to him. And at home in Italy, Zanni and his companions have enriched that other great indigenous dramatic form, the opera.

Opera was invented in Florence in about 1600, when several enterprising musician-poets began experimenting with dramas set to music. Until then, the Italian genius for singing had expressed itself in other forms of vocal music, ranging from the Mass to madrigals. Soon, Claudio Monteverdi, composer to the court of Mantua and later master of music in Venice, took up the new musical drama. In his operas, based on classical stories, such as the legend of Orpheus, the music responds to every twist in the plot, every change of mood. When Monteverdi had demonstrated what could be done with "the passionate style," as he called it, the rest of Italy quickly adopted opera as a favorite national pastime.

Before long, there were opera houses in even the smallest towns and cities, filled with audiences who were avid for new works and as fervent about opera as modern teenagers are about rock groups. No other country could boast such enthusiastic and knowledgeable music lovers. They provided the economic base for the steady stream of new operas that began to flow from the pens of dozens of Italian composers. The French novelist Stendhal arrived in Italy in 1800 with Napoleon's armies and marveled at the excitement that opera generated there.

Whenever an opera was to be performed, even in a small town, Stendhal observed, it seemed that the entire population was talking about it for days in advance. On the night of the production, the theater would be filled to the bursting point. Crowds would come pouring into town from miles around; all rooms at the inns would be taken, and some people would be obliged to camp out in their carriages while waiting for the doors of the theater to open. "The passions, the anxieties, the whole life of a thriving community is focused on its theater."

Stendhal compared the passionately

4

Carabinieri, **members of one of Italy's three police forces, display their blue and scarlet finery. The military dash of their full-dress uniform has changed little since its introduction in 1814. On regular duty, the division dresses in subdued, but well-cut, blue.**

committed audience at an Italian premiere with the blasé operagoers of Paris, who were accustomed to sitting on their hands and looking sideways at their neighbors to see how others were responding to the music. In Italy, "When the overture begins you could hear a pin drop. When it ends the storm bursts: The work is either extolled to the skies or sent to perdition with whistles and catcalls."

The darling of the audiences in Stendhal's time was Gioacchino Rossini, who wrote more than 40 operas — the best of which are comedies — in just over two decades. He was only 24 when he brought forth his masterpeice, *The Barber of Seville,* in 1816. By his own account, it took him 16 days to set down the score. The music seems to move with the same speed and fluency with which it was written; it bubbles and seethes with high jinks and satire. Much of the action is descended in a direct line from the *commedia dell'arte.* Figaro, the barber of the title, who by the end of the opera has become the factotum of Count Almaviva, is a valet figure in the Harlequin mold, endowed with all the cunning and eloquence of his *commedia dell'arte* original. He has an answer for everything — except his own troubles.

It was not Rossini's method to spend much time on sketches, revisions or adjustments. Nearly everything he composed was ready to be performed — or printed — the moment it left his pen. His recipe for writing an overture to an opera was: "Wait until the eve of the performance. Nothing stimulates the inspiration more than sheer necessity, the presence of a copyist who is waiting for your work, and the insistence of a frantic impresario who is tearing out his hair by the handful."

One desperate impresario locked

Rossini into a room with a plate of pasta and swore not to let him out until he had completed the overture to *Otello.* The overture to *Count Ory* was composed while Rossini was fishing, with his feet in the water. "With the *Barber,*" Rossini admitted, "I did not compose an overture at all, but took the one intended for the opera *Elizabetta.* The public was quite satisfied." He wrote the overture to *The Thieving Magpie* on the day of the premiere in a room under the eaves of La Scala, Milan's opera house. "I was guarded by four stagehands, who had instructions to throw my manuscript out of the window page by page — down to the copyists who were waiting below to transcribe it."

Two of Rossini's immediate successors, Vincenzo Bellini and Gaetano Donizetti, focused their efforts on the melodies in their operas, in order to give virtuoso singers the opportunity for dazzling technical displays. But in the mid-19th century, Giuseppe Verdi took opera into another psychological dimension: In the dramatic intensity of his music, he "crossed the frontier line that it is impossible to define, but beyond which beauty dwells," as the Russian novelist Ivan Turgenev once wrote about a Venetian performance of Verdi's *La Traviata.*

Verdi was to become the living embodiment of Il Risorgimento: In shouting *"Viva Verdi!,"* crowds of patriotic operagoers could also express their covert loyalty to the king whom they expected to bring about the reunification of their country, Vittorio Emanuele, *Re d'Italia.* At the same time, Verdi's music touched a singularly responsive chord in the Italian imagination. Turgenev reported that *La Traviata* left the performers as entranced as the audience. The singer playing the

role of the heroine who dies of consumption in the final moment of the opera had "tears of joy and real suffering in her eyes," said Turgenev. "Her face became transformed, and as the grim phantom of rapidly approaching death confronted her, the words *('morir s'i giovane!',* or 'to die so young!') were torn from her in a prayer of such passionate appeal to divine mercy that the whole theater shook with frenzied ap-

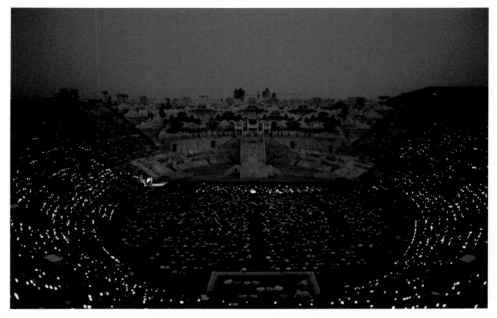

plause and rapturous cries."

After Verdi's string of successes with such heroic subjects as *Rigoletto, Aida* and *Otello,* it remained for Giacomo Puccini to round out the great tradition with turn-of-the-century operas such as *La Bohème* and *Tosca.* His plots acquired the label *verismo* — realism — because they dealt not with kings, dukes and generals but with artists, peasants and bohemians, performing passionate actions that were taken, more or less,

from life rather than from storybooks.

Puccini's incessant search for new theatrical effects and unusual settings led him to Japan, for *Madame Butterfly,* to China, for *Turandot,* and even to the American frontier, for *La Fanciulla del West* (The Girl of the Golden West), an opera whose heroes and villains are singing cowboys and whose heroine is a sort of Annie Oakley; Puccini even experimented with the idea of having eight or 10 horses onstage.

This was the furthest realism was pushed in Italian opera, and it was not a great success; *La Fanciulla del West* almost disappeared from the repertoire after its premiere in 1910. Since then, no composer of Puccini's stature, realist or otherwise, has emerged to contribute to the genre.

But the operatic tradition has remained very much alive in Italy, thanks in part to the crop of first-rate singers

Waiting for Puccini's *Turandot* to begin, operagoers in Verona hold lighted candles that outshine the night sky. Spectacular productions in the acoustically perfect Roman amphitheater attract international artists to a summer season of opera and ballet.

Two millennia meet in the Sicilian town of Agrigento, where the Greek Temple of Concord is silhouetted against the modern high-rise skyline. The early Christians converted the temple to a church, thereby sparing it the damage that befell most other monuments of the town's pagan past.

Milan's vast cathedral, built entirely of pearly white marble, dominates the city's main square. Created by more than 40 architects over a period of four centuries, it was begun in 1386 at the behest of Gian Galeazzo Visconti, the ruler of the duchy.

that each generation produces. The Neapolitan tenor Enrico Caruso (1873-1921) possessed one of the most beautiful voices that the opera world has ever known. Luciano Pavarotti, Mirella Freni and Katia Ricciarelli are among today's stars. When promising voices have served their apprenticeship in the provincial opera houses, they go on to bigger and better things abroad, returning for frequent performances at what has remained the very shrine and stronghold of Italian opera — the theater of La Scala, Milan.

Opera is still a part of popular culture in Italy as nowhere else in the world. Audiences treat singers with the enthusiasm usually reserved for sports and rock figures, cheering and jeering and commenting on their performance, much as they did in Stendhal's day. Even the smaller cities still have their opera houses. In the summertime in Verona, Spoleto, Naples, Rome — where the stage is nestled in the ruins of the Roman Baths of Caracalla — there is opera out of doors, and the night sky adds its luster to the setting.

While their commitment to opera remains steadfast, modern-day Italian audiences display an equally strong passion for the movies. Their devotion is understandable: During the past 40 years, many of the nation's best creative talents have expressed themselves on film. In the early postwar years, Italians won international renown with their so-called neorealist films, portraying the drama and tragedy of everyday life. Roberto Rossellini's *Roma Città Aperta (Open City)* inaugurated the style in 1945 with stunning performances by Anna Magnani and Aldo Fabrizi. The movie's strength and verisimilitude were due in part to its having been shot on the streets of war-weary Rome. Another powerful film was Vittorio de Sica's *The Bicycle Thief,* which related the misadventures that befell an honest laborer when his bicycle was stolen.

Other gifted film makers were drawn to satire and surrealism. Federico Fellini's *La Dolce Vita* was something of a milestone: It served up what was supposedly a slice of modern Roman life, replete with sex, cynicism and sacrilege — with Anita Ekberg as a voluptuous movie star dressed at one point in a monsignor's hat and cassock.

Thereafter, Fellini directed a series of imposing films in which he combined private dreams with apocalyptic commentaries on contemporary society. The most highly praised was *8½,* which concerned a director who was unable to choose the subject of his next film. It unfolded at a breathless pace in a succession of dreams, daydreams, memories — many abounding in visual satire that might easily have fitted into a *commedia dell'arte.* The title itself holds a mirror to Fellini's dilemma in making the film. The director originally adopted the title as a sort of opus number: He had shot seven and a half films before that, and he could not think of any better name for his latest work.

Luchino Visconti began his directing career as a neorealist, but eventually opted for the gorgeously costumed world of the historical epic. His finest films include *Il Gattopardo (The Leopard),* based on Giuseppe Tomasi di Lampedusa's novel about an aristocratic family coming to terms with the new order in Risorgimento Sicily, and a glittering, moody adaptation of Thomas Mann's *Death in Venice.*

Among the other distinguished Italian film makers of the most recent generation are Michelangelo Antonio-

ni and Bernardo Bertolucci. Antonioni's film *Blow-Up* took a telescopic and wide-angle view of the fascinating world of the modern British fashion photographer: The intricate plot unwound to the accompaniment of hectic action and sexual fireworks. Bertolucci made his reputation with *Last Tango in Paris,* a film that exploited the talents of Marlon Brando as an aging American caught in a web of passion with a clinically detached young Frenchwoman.

Last Tango in Paris has some of the qualities that epitomize the best Italian movies — visual splendor and psychological acuteness. Whether they deal with aspects of political history or the convolutions of the human psyche, Italian movie directors seem to look at life with the sweeping perspective of men and women who have grown up alongside real Roman temples and not the papier-mâché kind.

The Italian film industry has also produced a spate of memorable actresses. Silvana Mangano emerged as the first of the postwar European sex symbols, to be followed soon afterward by Gina Lollobrigida and Sophia Loren, who was voted the world's most popular female star in 1969. The tradition of the Italian golden girl has since been upheld by Ornella Muti, among others. Of Italian male leads, no name ranks higher than Marcello Mastroianni's, although some other male stars, notably Ugo Tognazzi, have made international reputations for themselves.

The majority of Italian films are made for internal consumption and remain unknown to the rest of the world. They deal with Italian themes — the lives of *mamma* and *papà,* provincial heartbreak romances, and so on — in ways that are more compelling and intelligible at home than abroad. Not

even Sophia Loren's persuasive presence was able to make most of her Italian movies exportable to the rest of Europe and the United States.

Italy's visual felicities, on the other hand, are appreciated by the whole of the Western world. As Stendhal said, Italy is a land where "the physical sensation of beauty is wafted at you from every side, like puffs of wind." Generations of its people, using their innate gifts for visual impact and theatrical display, have enhanced nature's handiwork with their own creations.

The Greek colonists in the south selected superb sites for the temples they built of golden stone. The ruins of Selinunte, in Sicily, provide a case in point: The massive Doric temple dominates a headland that affords a panoramic view of the sea.

While carrying on many of the Greek

4

architectural traditions, the Romans developed a novel style of their own, using monumental vaults and domes. Rome is full of great public buildings — temples, theaters, triumphal arches — raised to testify to its glory. After the Roman Empire vanished, its buildings remained as a challenge and inspiration to the centuries that followed.

Gradually, the arts of the ancient Roman world were adapted to suit the requirements of medieval Italy. The Romans had decorated their villas at Pompeii and Herculaneum with mythological idylls or with scenes from their favorite plays. Medieval builders adorned their churches with glittering mosaics of the saints and the Godhead, or they covered the walls with frescoes. The tradition of painting churches with the stories of the saints to which they were dedicated provided cities and towns the length and breadth of the country with their own treasure houses of ecclesiastical art.

But toward the end of the medieval period, paintings in this tradition lost their conviction and power; their practitioners were content to follow the old formulas mechanically, without feeling for the subject. As a reaction to this decline, the artists of the wealthy cloth merchants' city of Florence began as early as the 13th century to rethink their aims and methods; and in the process, they inaugurated that astonishingly fruitful epoch in the history of art, the Renaissance.

To imitate nature, and even to improve on it, was the aspiration of the Florentine innovators, and their central concern was to create a new image of man. To this end, they studied human anatomy, the science of optics and the laws of perspective. They also turned for inspiration to the classical art of Greece and Rome — works that were never quite forgotten but for centuries had been virtually ignored. In the heroic proportions and poses of the ancient statues, Renaissance artists recognized the idealized human being, the improvement on nature. Psychological truth mattered to them as much as convincing forms, and in their portrayal of human emotions and interactions, these artists surpassed anything in the classical canon.

In the early Florentine Renaissance of the 14th and 15th centuries, sculpture was first among the arts — understandably enough, since an object modeled in the round seems closer to nature than a flat, painted surface. One of the greatest sculptors of his day was Lorenzo Ghiberti (1378-1455), who devoted the better part of his life to creating two pairs of monumental bronze doors — "compositions rich with many figures" — for the baptistery of Florence's cathedral. Ghiberti was a passionate collector of Roman antiquities. He took his techniques from the Romans: They had developed bronze sculpture into a major art, but in the intervening centuries it had almost disappeared. Ghiberti borrowed many of his motifs, too, from pagan sources, but he adapted them to Biblical subject matter and suffused his

work with the Christian spirit. A century later, Michelangelo said that Ghiberti's second set of doors was worthy to stand at the gates of paradise.

Michelangelo's own creations were influenced not only by all that had gone before him in the Renaissance but also by archeological finds. During his lifetime, from 1475 to 1564, the art collections of the popes were constantly being enlarged by ancient masterpieces, such as the *Laocoon,* unearthed near the Baths of Titus in 1506. Created by Greek sculptors in the first century B.C., the *Laocoon* group depicts the legendary priest of Apollo who, with his sons, is attacked by serpents as punishment for disobeying the god.

Michelangelo's later work was powerfully influenced by the *Laocoon's* dramatic theme of human suffering, expressed in histrionic gestures of despair. He applied the same theatricality to sculptures, such as *The Struggling Captive,* and to his most famous painting of Biblical subjects, the ceiling of the Sistine Chapel and its breathtaking companion piece, the *Last Judgment.*

All three of the leading artists of the High Renaissance — Leonardo da Vinci, Michelangelo and Raphael — were vitally interested in the problem of how to express human character in art. Leonardo was determined to "paint the face in such a way that it will be easy to understand what is going on in the mind." When he created the *Last Supper,* his great mural in Milan, he focused on the differing reactions of the 12 disciples at the dramatic moment when Christ announces that one of them is about to betray him. Raphael, the youngest of the three artists, was master of the large-scale narrative composition, but also possessed an extraordinary gift for portraiture.

Michelangelo's heroic *David* embodies the virile confidence of Florence: In 1504, the republic erected the 13-foot-tall statue in its main piazza. Michelangelo was only 29 when he completed the marble figure, which established him as by far the greatest sculptor of his generation.

4

Expressiveness remained one of the hallmarks of Italian art during the centuries that followed the High Renaissance, when both the subjects and their treatment became increasingly melodramatic. By their flamboyant use of light and shade, late-16th-century painters, such as Caravaggio, depicted scenes from the lives of the saints as though they were taking place onstage under theatrical lighting. A German critic, Johann Mattheson, remarked in 1728, toward the end of the Baroque era, that "the whole world has become a giant theater"; and it was the Italians who led the way, not just in painting but also in the exuberant design of their churches and palaces.

In Rome, the High Baroque is exemplified by the work of Gianlorenzo Bernini, the prodigious 17th-century architect and sculptor who left a stronger imprint on the city than any other individual artist. Rome is replete with monuments, loggias and ornamental sculpture created by Bernini; with churches, chapels, altars and tombs designed by Bernini; with bridges, courtyards and façades decorated by Bernini. The two immense semicircular colonnades in front of the great Basilica of St. Peter's are Bernini's handiwork, as are many of the most striking details in St. Peter's itself, including the massive bronze canopy over the main altar, which is supported by corkscrew-twisted columns.

Southern Italy also provided fertile ground for Baroque sculpture and painting. Here, an extravagant realism held sway: The villa of the prince of Palagonia, near Palermo, was guarded in the 18th century by six colossal statues of halberdiers and approached along a vast avenue flanked by sculpted monsters. For a landscape garden in Caserta, near Naples, the 18th-century sculptor Vanvitelli created a life-size tableau depicting the legendary hunter Actaeon's encounter with the goddess Diana and her entourage. Clusters of elegant marble figures seem to move freely against a background of rocks and cascading water.

Meanwhile, in the northeast, the artists of Venice had developed a distinct school of their own. Never as intellectual as the Florentines in their approach to painting, the Venetians of the 15th and 16th centuries beguiled the eye with their rich harmonies of color, the romantic landscapes in which their compositions are set, and the element of mystery that suffuses their works. Titian was the greatest artist among them; he drew upon the example of his predecessors Bellini and Giorgione and, in turn, provided inspiration for Veronese and Tintoretto. After a lull in the 17th century, the 18th century witnessed another flowering of Venetian art. Tiepolo decorated ceilings with a rococo lightness of touch and dizzy use of foreshortening; Canaletto's topographical pictures look almost like stage sets.

For a while, Italian art seemed to mark time while the nation preoccupied itself with the turbulent political events of the 19th century. But at the beginning of the 20th century, the members of a new movement, who called themselves Futurists, played a significant part in preparing Europe for the advent of modern art. The Futurists were the most theatrical art revolutionaries of the day. Beginning in 1909, their ideological leader Filippo Marinetti created an incendiary new vocabulary with his manifestoes. "A racing car whose hood is adorned with great pipes," he proclaimed, "is more beautiful than the *Victory of Samothrace.*" His audiences were indignant at the belittling of the sculpture of the Greeks, but Marinetti pressed on unabashed. Museums were "cemeteries" and it was time to tear them down. "Turn aside the canals to flood the museums! Oh, the joy of seeing the glorious old canvases bobbing adrift on those waters, discolored and shredded!"

Of course, most of this was merely clever propaganda, taken seriously only by the nihilist fringe that later followed Mussolini. In fact, Marinetti's artist-disciples, such as Carrá, Balla and Severini, produced a fascinating body of Futurist art that now hangs peacefully in the museums alongside the works of earlier centuries, which Marinetti had previously scorned.

Italy boasts some of the richest museums and galleries in the world, but most of its artistic heritage is to be seen in a more natural context. Paintings still hang in the churches and monasteries that commissioned the artists hundreds of years ago, and famous sculptures adorn working fountains. This is the way Italians like it: They prefer not to treat their mementos as exhibits that can only be seen under glass. Their traditional procedure is to incorporate the past and the present by grafting new branches onto the root stock of their civilization.

Just as the characters of the *commedia dell'arte* appear again and again in movies and operas, so the architects of the Christian era built on the foundations — or within the walls — of ancient temples. The whole of Rome is dotted with such recycled classical buildings. The church of Santa Maria sopra Minerva, for example, is built, as the name reveals, on the remains of a temple of

Minerva. The colossal mausoleum of the Emperor Hadrian became the Vatican's main fortress, the Castel Sant'Angelo, but now leads yet another existence as a museum — with a restaurant on the battlements.

In the former Theater of Marcellus, begun by Julius Caesar, is the palace of the Orsini — one of the great aristocratic families of Rome and effectively its rulers for long periods during the Middle Ages. The Orsini implanted their Renaissance palace above several rows of ancient stone arches: The extra height affords them one of the finest views of the Capitoline Hill. A small café, a tobacco shop and a shoe wholesaler incongruously now occupy the imposing structure. No one considered it strange that a princely family should live above a neighborhood café.

Next door there is the tiny church of Sant'Angelo in Pescheria, wholly encased in what was once the Portico of Octavia — a gift to his sister from Augustus, the first emperor, who liked to boast that he had found Rome a city of bricks and left it a city of marble. The walls of the church consist of Augustus' columns with the spaces between them filled with a stucco-covered mixture of bricks and rubble. During the 1980s, one of the Catholic youth movements began to use this church-within-a-monument to celebrate the Mass with hand clapping and shout-

4

ing, accompanied by electric guitars instead of an organ, and introducing folk rhythms that were borrowed from American gospel music. This, too, reflects the Italian genius for adaptation and renewal that has, over the centuries, accounted for the cultural continuity of both church and state.

Historians have pointed out that one reason the conversion from paganism to Christianity went so smoothly is that the early Christians displayed a remarkable capacity for absorbing and preempting existing customs and festivals, for finding something useful in the old formulas that could be applied to new purposes. In art as in religion, however, the new purpose often destroys the old. Much of the marble that was used in the mosaic floors of so many medieval Roman churches, for example, was completely stripped from classical buildings. During the 12th and 13th centuries, whole families of artists and craftsmen specialized in recycling the marble and porphyry of ancient Rome, sawing it into thin sections to produce mosaic floors, columns, thrones, altars, tombs and baldachins. Two exponents of this field, called Cosma, lent their name to all the others, who became known as the Cosmati.

Present-day Italians sometimes appear to accept their artistic heritage as casually and with as little respect as did the Cosmati. They will proudly announce that their cities are the best in the world, but — as is the case in other industrialized nations — they come close to ruining them with their love for automobiles, which clog the narrow medieval streets and choke the spacious piazzas. The shores of the incomparable Bay of Naples are littered with plastic bottles and other flotsam. Paintings

The crowds crossing St. Mark's Square are squeezed onto an emergency causeway of planks by one of Venice's recurrent floods. In winter, the worst season for *acqua alta* — high water — the city keeps platforms stacked close at hand in the squares.

106

in the churches are rarely well tended. In the years that followed World War II, Italian builders ravaged the landscape: Speculative construction created high-rise deserts on the outskirts of some of the most beautiful cities, and much of the finest coastline became a mass of concrete apartment houses. Few voices were raised in protest against this development.

But the problem lies not so much in public indifference as in the scale of the effort that would be required to preserve all of the nation's heritage. Italy possesses a greater concentration of art treasures than any other country, and a colossal program would be needed to give each one ideal treatment. Some instances reveal that Italians do care about their cultural legacy, and have always done so.

The indefatigable Bernini, for example, once overreached himself: He gilded the lily by adding two small bell towers to the perfect proportions of the domed Pantheon, another of the pagan temples that had been transformed into a Christian church. The people of Rome were very decided in their opinions of Bernini's efforts: They had liked the building better without the additions, which they dubbed "donkey's ears." After two centuries of complaints, the offending bell towers were pulled down so that the Pantheon could stand once again in its classical rotundity.

Preservationists are given a hearing in 20th-century Rome as well. The city has maintained the low skyline of its historic center by means of stringent building regulations and has spent agonizing decades constructing its subway system, because the bulldozers keep revealing archeological artifacts that ought to be excavated.

Florence provides a dramatic instance of Italians coming to grips with conservation. Floods in November 1966 — when the Arno River burst its banks — caused grievous damage to pictures, sculptures and buildings. Even as the river was rising, the curators and art specialists struggled waist-deep in water to remove threatened paintings from the flooded museums; thanks to their courageous efforts, many important works were saved from destruction. Thousands of other pieces, however, were either destroyed or severely damaged. Yet the rescue operations that continued afterward were impressive. Italian specialists collaborated with teams of experts sent from other countries, which also raised large sums for the repair of paintings and library archives. The damaged buildings were lovingly restored by local masons and artisans.

On the very day that Florence was inundated, Venice suffered the worst floods of its history. The storms that filled the Arno to overflowing also whipped up the Adriatic; Venice was submerged under six and a half feet of water. Venice's crisis, unlike Florence's, could not be mitigated by a once-and-for-all preservation effort — for, tragically, the 1966 inundation was only one of many that were rapidly rotting away the fabric of the city. Floods became more and more frequent in the course of the 1960s and early 1970s.

The cause of the watery onslaught was twofold. Because of the shifting of the earth's crust, the sea was rising; meanwhile, the islands on which Venice is built were sinking. With their stone houses built on wooden piles and mud, Venetians have had to cope for centuries with subsidence. The situation, however, deteriorated rapidly in

the decades after World War II, when industries on the mainland began pumping huge quantities of water from beneath Venice's lagoon, thus lowering the water table and compacting the soil. The same industries also polluted the air with chemicals that gnawed away at Venice's buildings and statues.

In the late 1960s, in the wake of the devastating flood, the world's biggest and most ambitious preservation effort was launched to save Venice. National societies from all over the world set about restoring individual buildings from the ravages of air and water. In the decade that followed, the Italian government virtually halted Venice's submersion by providing a new supply of water for the city and, more importantly, for the mainland industries threatening it. Huge aqueducts were built to carry ample supplies from the rivers that feed the lagoon to the points of use; now that pumping from beneath the lagoon has ceased, the water table has returned to its natural level.

Venice still needs protection, however, from the high tides that immerse it several times a year. Moves to erect flood barriers at the entrances to the lagoon foundered repeatedly against bureaucratic inertia and the violent disagreements of all the experts who were called in to assess the gigantic engineering problems raised. At last, however, plans to build a set of movable flood barriers are under consideration. If approved, the project will take many years to complete, but there is every reason to believe that science will conspire with politics to preserve this unlikeliest of communities — "a city of rose and white," as the British painter J.M.W. Turner described it, "rising out of an emerald sea against a sky of sapphire blue." □

FIGURES IN AN IMMEMORIAL LANDSCAPE

The landscapes and cityscapes of Italy have been indelibly engraved on the consciousness of the Western world through the works of the nation's great artists. The golden age of Italian landscape painting lasted only a few decades, from the mid-15th to the early 16th century. At that time, the scientific currents of the Renaissance were encouraging artists to observe nature and record what they saw. In consequence, the background settings of both religious and secular paintings became increasingly naturalistic. Later, in the High Renaissance of the 16th century, painters rejected the idea of merely reproducing what was before them; they intensified and idealized every element of a picture, including the background.

Today, much of Italy remains as it was was when recorded by such Early Renaissance painters as Piero della Francesca and Antonio Pollaiuolo. Travelers can still encounter the cypress-clad slopes of Tuscany, the conical hills of Umbria and the bustling waterways of Venice that they have seen depicted in the world's galleries.

But the traveler's sense of recognition is in part an illusion, for even in the Early Renaissance, artists did not slavishly depict nature. Rather, they assembled their pictures from different elements, some drawn from life and others from artistic conventions. The illuminated manuscripts of the medieval period provided one source of idealized mountains and lakes, and the works of northern European artists, such as the van Eycks, were also becoming influential in Italy. In the painting on the right by the Venetian artist Giovanni Bellini, for example, the acutely observed castle and fields in the wintry Po valley are set against distant mountains inspired by Flemish models. Bellini has bathed the entire landscape in early-morning light, thus blending it into a harmonious whole.

Giovanni Bellini's *Virgin of the Meadow* (1510) contemplates her child in a landscape of harmony and eternal stillness. Bellini was a member of the first generation of Italian artists to use oil paint, which, with its translucency and rich color, lent a new verisimilitude to depictions of nature.

Vittore Carpaccio's *Miracle of the Holy Cross* (1494) depicts a crowded scene at the Rialto, Venice's mercantile center. The wood bridge was the forerunner of the stone Rialto Bridge, which was built in 1590 and still stands today. The miracle, the curing of a madman, is relegated to the loggia on the left.

In *The Martyrdom of St. Sebastian* (1475) by the Pollaiuolo brothers, the saint suffers at the hands of his tormentors in a landscape reminiscent of the Arno valley near Florence, though the far mountains are imaginary. The arch may symbolize Rome, where Sebastian, a soldier, died for his faith in 288 A.D.

CLARVS INSIGNI VEHITVR TRIVMPHO ·
QVEM PAREM SVMMIS DVCIBVS PERHENNIS ·
FAMA VIRTVTVM CELEBRAT DECENTER ·
SCEPTRA TENENTEM

Piero della Francesca's *Triumph of Federigo da Montefeltro* (1466) shows the Duke of Urbino and his wife *(right)* in

QVE MODVM REBVS TENVIT SECVNDIS ·
CONIVGIS. MAGNI DECORATA RERVM ·
LAVDE GESTARVM VOLITAT PER ORA ·
CVNCTA VIRORVM ↝

allegorical procession through the Umbrian countryside. An inscription on a stone parapet in front describes the event.

In Leonardo da Vinci's *Annunciation* (1472), the daisies and lilies in the foreground are rendered with scientific accuracy. But Leonardo refined the silhouettes of the cypresses behind the angel into near-perfect geometric forms; and the mountain is fantasy, conveying the unattainable sublime.

THE EBULLIENT ECONOMY

A visitor to a typical industrial country catches hardly a glimpse of its economy in action; hidden away in industrial parks and blocks of office buildings, manufacturing and business remain abstractions. In Italy, however, the economy is tangible: A visitor encounters it in every side street. Workshops turn out machine tools, knitwear, jewelry or gloves; markets sell the produce of small gardens; bars and restaurants appear at every corner. Italy is one of Europe's economic heavyweights, and its gross domestic product is ranked among the world's top seven. Yet with innumerable home industries spilling onto their pavements, parts of Italy's cities have almost the atmosphere of an Oriental bazaar.

With the small scale of Italy's most typical ventures goes a pattern of life that is unfamiliar to other industrial countries. Whereas Americans and Northern Europeans prefer to get their work done briskly or grimly before settling down to leisure and family life, Italians live their lives around their work and involve their families in it. To an outsider their attitude seems carefree, perhaps even too casual: An artisan will interrupt his labors for extended meals, long siestas, vigorous conversation. But the same artisan will be back at his bench to labor until sunset in the cool of the day, and his brothers and cousins will probably be there too, working beside him.

In Italy, there are about one million manufacturing enterprises with an average number of only seven employees, and many more equally small outfits offering services of one sort or another. These small businesses are the Italian economy's great strength. Families working for themselves are motivated to make a success of their venture; they will cheerfully put in long hours and go without immediate rewards for the sake of tomorrow. Their operations, moreover, are more flexible than those of large concerns; with limited stocks and low capital outlays, small-scale entrepreneurs can move in a new direction as soon as they sense a change in the market.

At the opposite end of the industrial ladder, Italy is the home of some of the world's most famous manufacturing brand names. Fiat, with an output that exceeds one million vehicles each year, is Europe's largest auto manufacturer. Olivetti is Europe's most enterprising creator of office equipment. Pirelli is one of Europe's leading tire makers. All three of these firms have international interests.

Giant enterprises and small businesses have transformed Italy's economy in only four decades. At the end of the Second World War, Italy was a poor agrarian nation without a tradition of trading on a large scale with other countries. Today, Italy exports a higher proportion of its manufactured goods than any other industrial country except West Germany. The average

Elegantly attired in a fur-trimmed leather cape, a woman pauses outside one of Florence's many jewelry shops. With its artistic heritage and its modern boutiques, the city typifies the unbroken tradition of fine design and craftsmanship that is one of the main assets of the Italian economy.

117

5

Italian family is twice as rich in real terms as it was just 25 years ago.

If this were the whole story, Italy would be a promised land, and the millions of Italians who exiled themselves in the years after World War II to escape grinding poverty would be rushing home to earn their fortunes instead of waiting to go back to the old country with their pensions. There are, however, darker aspects to the Italian economy. One of them is the uneven distribution of the new wealth.

Industry is concentrated in an inverted triangle of territory that covers Turin, Venice and Leghorn. Within this area, and indeed throughout the north, people live as well as anywhere in Europe. Below Tuscany and Umbria, the standard of living is lower. Milan, the commercial heart of the north, may have outskirts scarred with factories and faceless low-cost housing, but the overall impression is of people making a lot of money and cheerfully spending it on anything the world can provide. In contrast, the city of Rome — less than 40 miles south of Umbria — is not as well off, though the capital is rich in art and history and has some fine shopping streets. Expensive stores are thinly spread, and the fabric of the place is less cared for.

Even in the north, however, the normally buoyant economy is likely to capsize into a sudden depression. One reason for the economy's precariousness is Italy's heavy reliance on imported energy. The country has little oil and only low-grade coal. Its resources of gas and hydroelectric power are sufficient to meet only one sixth of its total energy needs. Two thirds of the fuel it uses is imported oil, and imported gas and coal make up another one sixth of consumption. Continued success at exporting their natural talents in the form of brilliantly designed cars or couture is crucial for the Italians, because it is only by selling abroad that they can afford to pay the enormous cost of imported fuel. And when world oil prices shoot up, the Italian economy rocks wildly.

Italy looks doomed to continue its dependency on imported oil for many years to come. There has been a move to build more nuclear power stations to boost the tiny proportion of electricity — just over 1 percent — produced at present by these means, but projects have been slowed by interminable local planning studies. A proposed switch to using more imported coal is held up because it would require heavy investment in coal ports and handling facilities at the points of consumption. Some relief is imminent from natural gas imported through an undersea pipeline that has been built between Italy and Algeria. The first supplies of natural gas flowed into the country in 1983, but the new resource did not immediately make a notable difference because local distribution pipelines were in short supply, and oil-burning power stations had yet to be converted to gas.

Another reason prosperity can never be taken for granted is conveyed in a recurring image of the Italian economy: a champion racehorse burdened with an overweight jockey. There is nothing wrong with the animal itself, which is swift and powerful when unencumbered. But the unfortunate creature is saddled with an onerous political and social system.

Italy's public sector has been more-or-less out of control for decades. Politicians use the large state-owned industrial sector — a legacy of the Fascists — as a machine for delivering votes through the construction of factories in depressed areas. The state-owned companies lose some three billion dollars a year because they employ too many people to make high-priced, low-quality goods that nobody wants. Financial management of essential public services, such as hospitals and schools, is often either inefficient or corrupt. The government never really knows how much it will end up having to borrow at home or abroad to balance its books at the end of the year.

Not surprisingly, Italy's public-sector deficit is the highest in the European league. Total government outstanding debt amounts to more than 80 percent of a year's output of the whole economy — compared with less than 60 percent in Britain and less than 50 percent in the United States.

Because the state preempts so much of the available capital, scarcity pushes up the price of money. Interest rates for loans rise, which makes it more difficult for private businesses to raise funds for growth. Thus the public deficit drives up the cost of doing business, and ultimately the cost of living. At almost any point since the mid-1970s, Italian inflation has been the highest among the world's major industrial countries. This in turn increases the cost of exports, making them less competitive in the world marketplace. The only solution is for the Italian lira to be devalued — but that also increases import prices and notches Italy's inflation up once more.

Every few years, sober-suited international bankers and economists from the International Monetary Fund (an organization that lends funds to countries with balance-of-payments problems) feel obliged to descend on Rome and start lecturing Italians and their politicians about living beyond their na-

A busy evening market fills the square
beside the church of San Michele in
the Tuscan town of Lucca. Italy's profusion of street markets, with family-
run stalls offering a small range
of goods, explains why it has the highest number of retailers in Europe — one
for every 60 people.

A CITY'S TRADITION OF VIOLIN CRAFTSMANSHIP

The curator of the violin collection in Cremona's city hall plays one of the instruments.

The town of Cremona in Lombardy has a special place in musical history. From the 16th to the 18th centuries, the finest violins the world has ever known were created in the city's workshops. Here, Andrea and Nicola Amati, Giuseppe Guarneri and the master of masters, Antonio Stradivari, made instruments of such miraculous tone that even today they are the choice of virtuosi. Some examples of the old violinmakers' art are housed in Cremona's city hall, and every morning one or two are played so that they retain the qualities built into them centuries ago.

But Cremona is not merely a repository of past glories. Tucked away in a warren of medieval streets are the studios of at least 50 master builders, some of whom teach their craft to students from more than 20 countries. Striving to reproduce the perfection of past eras, they take pains with every detail of the complex construction process.

Each violin is composed of 72 pieces of wood of at least seven types — chiefly maple, for the hard back and neck of the instrument, and spruce, for the soft front. The wood is aged for up to 10 years, in which time it dries slowly and evenly. After the lengthy work of cutting and gluing, the violins are seasoned for a year.

The final stage in a violin's creation — one vitally important for its timbre — is the application of 30 layers of varnish. Each coat dries in the open air, and one of the characteristic sights of Cremona is lines of violins hanging above the roofs like washing. The master builders who use traditional methods average five to six violins a year, of which 90 percent are exported at around $10,000 each.

Stradivari is immortalized in stone.

After applying glue, an artisan clamps the body of a violin.

Varnish dries on violins hanging among Cremona's rooftops. Below, blocks of wood are propped against a parapet for seasoning.

5

tional means. When things get really bad, the Bank of Italy takes drastic measures. It slams the brakes on the economy by reducing the supply of money and credit available to either the government or the private sector. The whole system slows down to a crawl until debts, price increases and the gap between exports and imports decline to more reasonable proportions. These periods of painful readjustment rarely seem to coincide with the recessions of the world's other industrialized countries, nor do Italy's bursts of exhilarating progress always coincide with boom years elsewhere. With its peculiar strengths and weaknesses, the Italian economy behaves like no other.

Both the strengths and the weaknesses have roots that extend far into the past. Since World War II, the strengths have far outweighed the weaknesses, but previously the opposite was true: For most of the 19th century, the obstacles in the way of industrialization seemed prohibitive. Because the cost of importing coal was prohibitively high, lack of energy sources was even more of a problem than it is in these oil-burning days. The political situation, moreover, discouraged taking risks. Centuries of foreign domination followed by the disturbances of Il Risorgimento left Italians with a strong preference for cautious, conservative investment in real estate. And, since there was no nationwide market before unification, any entrepreneur would have found it hard to sell his goods in Italy; even afterward, much of the population was too poor to buy industrial products.

On the other hand, Italy's human resources constituted a strength that would eventually enable these handicaps to be overcome. Many rural peo-

ple were part-time artisans who could draw upon a long tradition of fine design and craftsmanship. Silk manufacture was a widespread cottage industry, producing one of Italy's main exports. In Venice, glassmaking skills that had developed over hundreds of years were still carefully nurtured.

Italians were also familiar with trade and finance. Venice and Genoa had been among the leading ports of the Mediterranean for centuries, and the Italian merchant fleet in the 19th century was one of Europe's largest. Italians invented banking in the 12th century, and by the 19th century, they had built up an extensive network of local finance houses. Italy also produced several distinguished scientists and inventors in the 19th and early 20th centuries — including Alessandro Volta, who made the first electric battery, and Guglielmo Marconi, who developed radio telegraphy.

From the 1870s onward, these varied talents began to be channeled into industry. Giovanni Pirelli built his first rubber-processing factory in Milan in 1872. The Olivetti enterprise dates from 1908, when the enlightened Camillo Olivetti located a typewriter factory at Ivrea in the clean air of the Piedmont hills and founded a model community on the outskirts of the town to house his workers.

In 1899, a group of industrialists led by Giovanni Agnelli, a former cavalry officer, created Fabbrica Italiana Automobili Torinto — called Fiat for short. By 1914, Fiat was producing more than 3,000 cars a year, and a clutch of other auto manufacturers — such as Alfa Romeo, Lancia and Bianchi — had also made international names for themselves with their engineering skills and stylish design. Italy

gradually became more prosperous, though it continued to lag behind the industrial giants of the day — Britain, Germany and the United States.

Industry was taking root only in the north of the country — indeed, most of it was concentrated around Milan, Turin and Genoa. The south was less able to convert its economy to an industrial one. It suffered from its position on the periphery of Europe; new ideas were slow to filter southward, export markets were hundreds of miles away. The manufacturing skills widespread in the north were lacking. The unification of Italy exacerbated the problems of the south by opening it up to competition with the north. The low level of industrialization in the south today is no accident: It is the almost-inevitable consequence of geography and history.

Mussolini became head of state in 1922. He was initially in favor of free trade, but after a few years, he declared *laissez-faire* economics to be out of date and set up a bureaucracy that intervened at every level of industry — and severely hampered its efficiency. In 1933, after several bank failures, Mussolini created the Institute for Industrial Reconstruction (IRI), whose function was to lend money to businesses in difficulty. Initially IRI's role was simply to restore ailing companies to health. But close supervision of industry corresponded with Mussolini's economic theories, and IRI soon became a permanent stockholder in the enterprises it bailed out. The result was that by 1939, the state, through IRI, controlled many of Italy's leading firms, especially in the steel, engineering, shipbuilding and banking industries.

Mussolini also attempted to direct agriculture, but with unfortunate results. Coaxing a living out of Italy's

Geothermal power station chimneys dominate the Tuscan town of Larderello. The area's volcanic geology traps steam in porous rock about half a mile underground. Dante described these steam vents in the *Divina Commedia;* today, they generate enough electricity to meet 1 percent of Italy's needs.

poor land had always been a struggle, and investment was rarely high enough to realize even the limited potential of the soil. The best results were obtained by growers of olives, grapes and fruit — crops that flourished even where rainfall was scanty and fields rocky. Instead of acknowledging that traditional crops fared best, however, Mussolini attempted to win agricultural self-sufficiency by waging a "battle for grain." Wheat production was duly increased, but only by growing the grain on land that was manifestly unsuitable for it — land where other crops would have succeeded. The miseries of the countryside worsened in the 1930s when Mussolini, fearing social unrest among the growing class of industrial workers, forbade migration from the country to the cities. As the countries of the Western Hemisphere imposed quotas on immigrants, cutting off the traditional escape route of rural Italians, more and more people became trapped in poverty.

After the war, when Italy set itself the task of industrializing rapidly, this particular problem transformed itself into a boon. In contrast to such countries as France and West Germany, Italy had an enormous potential labor force on its own small farm plots. The postwar generation that came out of the fields was prepared to work for low wages. But more and more factory workers were joining one of the labor unions, all of which had political affiliations. The largest union group was linked to the Communist and Socialist parties, the second-largest to the Christian Democrat party, and the third to several of the small political parties. However, ideological differences among the three camps sapped the bargaining power of the labor unions.

5

No other country could boast both an enormous untapped labor force and the inventive skills that Italy had already demonstrated. Shrewdly assessing his nation's potential just after the end of World War II, Vittorio Valletta, the president of Fiat, described Italy as the "engineering granary of Europe." Indeed, within a very few years, Italy was proving his claim.

Italy's economic miracle lasted from 1945 to the late 1960s. In the early years, the economy received a tremendous boost in the form of foreign aid — first from the Allied invasion forces and, after 1948, from the United States government, which provided funds, industrial equipment and know-how under the Marshall Plan.

By the start of the 1950s, the Italian economy was growing at a rate of more than 5 percent a year, and the nation managed to sustain that hectic pace throughout the next two decades. Most of Italy's growth was to be found in medium-technology manufacturing — cars, home appliances and plastics — but civil engineering and tourism also were taking off.

In France and Japan, the only other populous countries to rival Italy's growth during these years, the direction of industrial development was determined by the central government. Italy's economic miracle was achieved with nobody in charge — and Italians were well aware that in their country the government was more likely to be a hindrance than a help. Being such a recent federation of states, and lacking both the French tradition of centralization and the cohesion of West Germany, Italy was poorly equipped to run a centrally planned economy. Mussolini's efforts in that direction had been unsuccessful, and it soon became apparent that postwar governments would not be able to accomplish the task either. Short-lived coalitions quickly became the norm.

However, it was not possible for Italian industry to launch itself without some assistance from the government. The sums of money required for initial capital investment were enormous by any reckoning, and at the end of World War II, Italy's financial system was so shaky that only the state could possibly commandeer the necessary credit. One of the great Italian achievements of the immediate postwar period was to devise a means by which industry could benefit from state resources without being damaged by government meddling. .

Paradoxically, the principal organization to have success in keeping the government-backed companies at arm's length from politicians was the one created by Mussolini for controlling industry — IRI. The agency was revived and given the task by government of developing basic heavy industries. IRI and the various subsidiaries it spawned duly founded modern steel, chemical and engineering enterprises. The government-backed industries were never entirely free from political pressure, but for a number of years this remained at a tolerable level. A similar body, the National Hydrocarbons Board (ENI), was established in 1953 to develop Italy's natural-gas supplies. It subsequently branched out into oil refining and the manufacture of petroleum products. And before long, the government had created additional holding companies with responsibility for particular industries.

Italy's lack of industrial infrastructure, which had looked to some like a disadvantage, quickly proved to be a blessing. Building heavy industry from scratch, Italy was able to follow the same growth pattern that Japan traced during the postwar period. The state-backed steel industry was developed in tandem with the privately controlled consumer-product industry, which was its biggest customer. The efficient steelmakers gave an enormous advantage to the producers of cars and refrigerators, who began to flood Europe with their low-priced products after Italy helped to set up the European Economic Community (EEC) in 1957. Successful automobile and appliance manufacturers, in turn, gave solid support to the steel industry, which was able to extend and improve its plants without having to worry about an economic return on investment.

The partnership between public and private companies worked beautifully; for years IRI and the other holding companies were cited throughout Europe as a model of beneficial government intervention in industry.

While IRI protected state enterprises from government, private firms had to devise their own methods to avoid attracting the attention of politicians — who might otherwise intervene on behalf of their constituents, for example, to insist that a factory be located in an unsuitable spot. There seemed to be two courses of action a company could take to stave off such unwelcome pressure. One solution was to shrink so small that it no longer interested politicians. The other was to grow large and powerful enough to be able to defy government's wishes. Thus, where economies of scale were not paramount, Italy developed its unique brand of decentralized production: the small businesses that are the most striking feature of Italian industry. At the same time, the

The Pirelli skyscraper, symbol of Italy's postwar boom, towers grandly in this panoramic view of Milan. Designed in the late 1950s by Gio Ponti, it now houses government offices for the Lombardy region.

big companies such as Olivetti and Pirelli grew ever larger.

The biggest private group of all was and continues to be Fiat, which not only dominates auto production in Italy but has long since diversified into such areas as mining, finance, newspapers and medical supplies. Italian journals love to run opinion polls on who the readers consider are the most powerful figures in Italy. Giovanni Agnelli, the leader of the family that still owns most of the shares in the Fiat empire founded by his grandfather, always comes out near the top of the list.

The immense influence of Fiat not only has cushioned the company from political interference but has earned it some special privileges, notably long-term restrictions on the import of Japanese cars. The arrangement was a reciprocal one, and it had first been suggested in the 1950s by the Japanese, who were alarmed at the prospect of a flood of Italian imports damaging their fledgling automobile industry. Even after Japanese auto manufacturing had reached maturity, however, the agreement between the two countries remained in force, contributing to Fiat's phenomenal growth. And the graceful city of Turin became increasingly dominated by the auto factories in its suburbs.

Although Turin and Fiat eventually became almost synonymous to most Italians, the city also exemplifies the opposite pole of the nation's industry. In the 1960s, while Fiat itself was growing, a vast development of engineering workshops — employing as many people as the auto factories themselves — spread in and around the city in order to supply the assembly lines. And in other cities throughout Italy similar growth was taking place.

DESIGNS OF WIT AND INTELLIGENCE

Italian mass-produced goods are renowned worldwide for their formal beauty, their brilliant coloring and their innovative solutions to functional problems. The Italian flair for design touches products as diverse as typewriters, sports cars and ballpoint pens, but it is in furnishings and fittings that it has made the greatest impact.

Immediately after World War II, Italy started to make a name for itself as a font of fresh design ideas. Many of the best designers of the 1950s and 1960s had trained as architects. Opportunities to create interesting buildings were few because of a shortage of capital, so they directed their talent toward the shaping of consumer goods and interiors. They established a method that endures: Designers work in independent groups, offering their services to many companies. Freed from worries over management and sales, the groups — many based in Milan — can concentrate on esthetics.

From the start, the design groups embraced high technology and new materials: Indeed, sleek creations in molded plastic epitomize the Italian style. Synthetics are invariably used for their own sake, not disguised as wood or stone. The futuristic table lamps grouped here illustrate the typically Italian approach to the high-tech potential of metal and plastic.

5

During the 1950s, import duties that had been in force since the 1930s were gradually removed from such products as textiles, clothing, leather, jewelry and ceramics. The resulting international competition was an extremely effective, if rather painful, stimulus to small Italian producers of these goods. The family businesses competed among themselves but they also cooperated with one another. Sometimes they would even subcontract work to rivals who had extra capacity; often they would join forces to launch collective marketing and advertising campaigns. Whether their output was luxury items or more modest products, these small producers were rarely content with the easily accessible local markets; they reached out to sell to Europe.

The economic success story of the 1950s and 1960s was marred only by the failure of large-scale industry to take root in the south of Italy. In 1950, a special bureau, called the Cassa per il Mezzogiorno, had been set up to finance development in Italy's less-developed regions. Most of the organization's huge funds, however, were spent on engineering projects such as highways and dams, which, though valuable, did not produce long-term employment and mainly benefited the engineering companies from the north that had won the contracts.

Few private manufacturers were keen to build factories in potentially low-profit areas. At the government's insistence, some of the state industries were located in the southern regions, notably Europe's largest steelworks at Taranto in Puglia. This massive, integrated seaside complex took in iron ore that had been inexpensively shipped across the world in bulk carriers, then turned out the steel needed by the auto and appliance factories in the north. But such a factory hardly touched the problem of rural employment. Built with state capital almost regardless of cost, it was so mechanized that it required only a small work force.

Had it been more labor-intensive, the Taranto complex probably would have had the same sort of troubles experienced by the state-owned Alfa Romeo company when it set up its Alfasud fac-

tory outside Naples. The Alfasud factory was dogged by frequent strikes, high absenteeism and low-quality finishing because the workers had no tradition of the disciplines of industrial life. The distance from the factory to its markets added high shipping charges to the high production costs, increasing the company's difficulties. With time, many of Alfasud's problems were solved, but the long struggle discouraged other companies from following in its footsteps.

Some southern cities, such as Naples, developed their own networks of small businesses to rival those of the north. But these activities were not enough to make use of all the surplus labor, and many southerners had little choice but to leave their homes in search of work. In the 1950s and 1960s, about three million workers went to other EEC countries; several times that number chose to travel to the north of Italy to work in the thriving factories. Unlike the southerners who remained at home, the migrants adjusted to the demands of the production line, and they worked as well as the native northerners. But they did not integrate easily into the social fabric of their new environment. The local inhabitants tended to shun them, and the southerners' sense of alienation was increased by inadequate housing.

While the southern migrants had special grievances, other factory workers were getting restive too. They could sense the vigorous momentum of the economy, and yet their paychecks remained small. Whereas the first generation of industrial workers had been acquiescent employees, their children — who were beginning to enter the work force — began to demand a larger share of the spoils for them-

selves. The age when Italy could rely on a docile labor force was over.

New trends in factory construction reflected the difficult times. Suddenly, instead of giant operations, medium-size plants accommodating about 700 workers were in vogue. The size limit was calculated so that managers could know most of the employees by name, which presumably would help to improve relations with an increasingly hostile work force. The medium-size firms did largely succeed in avoiding trouble — but meanwhile, in the massive older companies, discontent increased. Left-wing extremists infiltrated many of the factories to apply their college-learned socialist theories by educating the masses in the exploitative nature of the capitalist system.

The worker's resentments eventually came to a head in the so-called hot autumn of 1969, when strikes and demonstrations paralyzed much of Italian industry for about a month. After a while, the employers gave in to the workers' demands and conceded unusually large wage increases. The following year, a new law — the Workers' Charter — was passed, which gave employees increased security in their jobs and spelled out the rights of labor unions within companies.

Their credibility boosted by these successes, the left-wing extremists in the labor unions set about creating anarchy in Italian factories. Over and over again, on the flimsiest of pretexts and without any warning, small groups of workers staged brief stoppages in the large automobile and engineering plants. The chaos caused by the unpredictable behavior of the workers damaged Italian industry far more than the extra costs incurred by management in

granting improved pay and conditions.

In 1973 and 1974, there was a different crisis to try Italian industry: the quintupling of oil prices in a matter of months as a result of decisions made by the OPEC cartel. The price increase put a spoke in the wheels of even the most stable of the Western economies, and Italy's economy, so dependent on energy imports, suffered more severely than most others. The annual inflation rate rose to 25 percent.

After four years of doing battle in the factories, the unions found themselves in a formidable position to protect their purchasing power when inflation took off. They won real wage hikes of about 10 percent from 1974 to 1975, and productivity stopped growing.

Next, taking advantage of the climate that prevailed in Italian politics, the unions succeeded in pushing through changes in the law that had the effect of more or less institutionalizing inflation. Since 1957, Italian workers had been partly sheltered from the declining value of money by a so-called escalator, which automatically raised their wages as prices rose. But in 1975, the unions managed to greatly extend their protection. All workers, regardless of their earnings, thenceforth received a flat sum that automatically compensated them for as much as 75 percent of the previous three months' price increases. In practice, this meant that wages went up even faster than the cost of living, because the better-paid groups fought for extra raises to maintain their differentials, and because various industries negotiated national and local wage deals in addition to the increments that everyone received.

Other European countries that tied wages to the cost of living during the 1970s were able to loosen the bonds by

Rows of umbrellas crowd an Adriatic beach at the height of the three-month summer season. Foreigners have flocked to the 300 miles of sand along Italy's eastern shore since the 19th century, but today they are outnumbered by native vacationers.

5

the end of the decade. But Italy had to wait until 1983 for wage indexing to be tackled by the Craxi government, which was willing to endure unpopularity with the labor unions. Even then, they did not shelve the system and introduced modifications instead. Automatic wage indexing was cut by 15 percent, but the principle remained.

In the 1970s, inflation combined with unrest in the factories to make Italian goods increasingly uncompetitive. Although the Fiat company was still protected from its Japanese rivals by import quotas, Italy's membership in the EEC prevented the nation from keeping out cars from other European countries. Fiat sales dropped considerably until the company retained barely half the domestic market it had traditionally dominated. In other European countries, Japanese and West German products were ousting Fiat from its position as market leader. Other large private Italian companies suffered a similar fate at home and abroad.

The unaccustomed experience of industrial failure diverted IRI and the other government bodies from their true purpose. As Third World countries began to develop steel and other heavy industries, offering fierce competition to Italy's strike-ridden firms, the country should logically have closed down some of its factories and redirected its work force. But the government was under intense pressure not to take such a drastic measure, however much sense it made economically. IRI became a convenient conduit for channeling taxpayers' money into failing businesses, avoiding the political cost of closing plants and putting people out of work. The agency was soon discredited.

No end to the problem seemed in sight, and official forecasts for the economy looked more and more bleak. But the official forecasters were concentrating their attention on the ailing industrial giants and forgetting the existence of the back-street economy: the hundreds of thousands of small firms that employed cheap, nonunion labor. Conventional wisdom at the time had it that labor-intensive industry was drifting away from Europe to the newly industrialized Southeast Asian countries and Latin America. But Italy proved that its labor-intensive businesses were still capable of competing internationally. In the late 1970s, the nation managed an extraordinary spurt of progress, growing faster between 1977 and 1980 than any other industrial country. The little firms were responsible for this dazzling performance.

But all the known small businesses could not account for the level of economic activity in Italy at the time. Something else was going on: a phenomenon that had already been noted and christened the "submerged," or "black," economy. A Rome sociologist, Giuseppe de Rita, first drew the public's attention to it in 1971. His social-research bureau obtained evidence that the official economic statistics were hopelessly wrong because they failed to record the output of thousands of manufacturing businesses. These enterprises were operating unseen on the margins of the economy, thereby escaping taxes, staying clear of union interference and avoiding expensive labor regulations. Instead of hiring a regular staff, these concealed cottage industries used self-employed consultants or homeworkers.

De Rita subsequently monitored the progress of the hidden sector, coming to the conclusion that it contributed 20 percent of Italy's economic output in the course of the 1970s. Unofficial economic activity has long existed, of course, in other countries; Italy was unusual because the unofficial sector was so large, and because it was chiefly concerned with making things rather than performing services — for example, cleaning windows or repairing cars. Some saw its workings as a brilliant exercise in capitalist adaptation; others saw it as a crude commerical exploitation of working people.

At the start of the 1980s, while small companies continued to prosper, giant concerns discovered a new lease on life. But in contrast to the days of the economic miracle, when state industries had been the pacesetters, the big private companies now showed the way for the rest of the economy. The turning point from the anarchy of the 1970s came in October 1980, when thousands of Fiat supervisors and middle managers marched through the streets of Turin to protest the latest in a long series of strikes by their fellow workers. The March of the 40,000, as it came to be known, symbolized the new mood of cooperation within industry. Workers and employers combined forces to bring about the transformation that quickly followed their action.

At Fiat, the Agnelli family stood back from the day-to-day managment and left the field clear for a new breed of technocrats. The company made huge investments in efficient means of production, such as robots. Absenteeism among the workers dropped, productivity rose, and the first new model of the 1980s, the Uno, was voted car of the year in 1984 by the European automotive press. The company regained most of the ground it had lost in and

An aqueduct crosses the dry landscape of Basilicata in southern Italy. In an attempt to develop the economically depressed south, the Italian government has financed the construction of an irrigation network that totals more than 9,300 miles.

outside Italy, and it soared back to regain the No. 1 auto-manufacturing position in Europe.

Olivetti staged an equally dramatic recovery at about the same time. The firm had nearly collapsed in the 1970s, primarily because its managers did not notice until late in the day that the microchip was rendering obsolete the carefully engineered mechanical innards of its electric typewriters. Losses had reached more than $100 million in 1978 when Carlo de Benedetti, a wealthy Piedmontese businessman, was brought in to reverse the trend. He had briefly held a top position with Fiat, but he had found the family atmosphere too pervasive. He put in $17 million of his own money to acquire a 20 percent holding in Olivetti. Benedetti then set about forming partnerships with French, American, Japanese and Canadian companies in order to get back both the products and the market share that years of neglect by previous management had allowed to slip.

The firm leaped from the age of the typewriter into the modern computerized office, introducing a range of products that included electronic telexes, desktop computers, word processors and terminals. Not only was this equipment as beautifully designed as people had come to expect of Italian products, but its systems and software were of top quality. The newly revived firm received an accolade in 1983 when the giant American Telephone and Telegraph company, seeking a European partner for its expansion in office electronics, chose Olivetti and bought a quarter share in the firm.

Similar recoveries were taking place elsewhere in the big private groups: for example, among large textile manufacturers. Italy had constructed the most modern synthetic-fiber plants in the world in the 1970s, at a time when global overproduction made the investment seem a financial disaster. But in the late 1970s, after factory closings everywhere — including Italy — because of slack demand, the up-to-date Italian plants began to reap the profits. Partly

Residents of Tuscany's Chianti hills crush grapes that have been partly dried in the sun after picking. For the family's supply of wine, they will follow local custom and will add this sugary pulp to the rest of the grapes as they ferment — to round out the flavor.

as a result of this success, clothing and textiles have crept up to No. 2 in the table of Italian manufactured exports, behind machinery. Some of the credit for this achievement, however, must go to the still-flourishing tradition of silk manufacture and to the brilliant Italian clothing designers, which, by the early 1980s, had made Milan the ready-to-wear fashion capital of the world.

Another industry that was hit in the 1970s, only to recover in the 1980s, was tourism. In the 1960s, Italy had vigorously promoted its sun and its sand, but Spain offered the same attractions at a lower price; by the 1970s, Spain was drawing the crowds away from Italy's beaches. Italy responded to the competition by marketing its unrivaled heritage of art and architecture, locating helpful tourist bureaus in every historic town and featuring itineraries chosen especially for the traveler interested in cultural pursuits. The results were dramatic. By the early 1980s, tourism was bringing in more foreign currency than any other industry in the Italian economy except machinery.

The new strength in major industries had a ripple effect on small firms. One sign of health was the emergence of clandestine businesses into the open. Giuseppe de Rita — who had brought the black economy to the attention of the world in 1971 — found, a decade later, that in places such as the textile town of Prato near Florence, the number of officially registered workplaces had doubled. De Rita reckoned that the real rate of job creation, though healthy, could not be as high as this, and he concluded that many of the apparently new companies had previously been part of the black economy. Some had emerged because they had grown to a point where the increasingly

vigilant tax collectors could spot them, while others appeared simply because the climate for enterprise had improved so much that there was no longer an overwhelming imperative to remain in hiding.

Only in the south, where the tax collectors had not yet made much progress, was the submerged economy thought to prevail. Around Naples, for example, millions of pairs of gloves were being turned out each year from an officially tiny number of factories, which could not possibly have been responsible for such a large output.

Although there undoubtedly are hidden pockets of enterprise in the south, the overall southern economy still lags

behind the north's. The government funds poured into development in the south over the past few decades have done little to lessen the economic gap between north and south.

Even in the north, however, there is no room for the workers to become complacent. Agriculture's fortunes have been mixed. The farming sector has rapidly shed much of its excess work force: 6.6 million people worked on the land in 1960, and by the mid-1980s, this number was reduced to 2.5 million. But the latter figure was 11 percent of the total Italian labor force, a much higher percentage than in other industrial countries. Even France, the EEC's other big agricultural employer, had only 8 percent of its working popu-

lation on the land in the mid-1980s.

The most efficient Italian farms are comparable to any in Europe. Overall, however, the degree of mechanization is low: Italy has only 46 tractors per 100 workers, for example, compared with nearly twice that in the other large EEC countries. The poor, hilly terrain continues to stand in the way of streamlined methods and large yields. The farming population is aging fast, and many people fear that as the old farmers retire from their struggles with the soil, their places will not be taken by members of the younger generation.

The most troubled part of the Italian economy, however, remains the state-owned sector. Losses in this area are still enormous. Painful decisions to close down steelworks have been made only very reluctantly.

Some of the large private companies have also had a difficult time. Several major kitchen-appliance manufacturers almost collapsed in the early 1980s. And their problems point to difficulties that may face a large segment of Italian industry. Most economists believe that the straightforward medium-technology manufacturing that played such a big part in the Italian economy of the 1960s will move to newly industrialized countries. In the meantime, the rich countries will develop high-technology production and ever more sophisticated services. To the extent that rich countries continue to make such goods as refrigerators, they will equip them with up-to-date electronics.

Olivetti excepted, Italian companies have not shown much affinity for complex electronics. The simpler sorts of electronic gadgetry are routinely incorporated in Italian machine tools, but Italians have not kept abreast of the most dazzling innovations. In Italian universities, there are very few chairs of information technology.

The biggest challenge for Italian industry now is to catch up rapidly in these crucial areas. Failure would put the entire engineering sector of Italian manufacturing at risk. But failure is far from inevitable. If the Italians exercise their customary ingenuity, they should look forward to an economic future as successful as their last few decades. □

Surrounded by bales of material
ready for reprocessing into new cloth,
a Prato textile worker sorts a pile of
rags into different colors and fibers.
The used fabrics will be saturated
with acid, then heated to destroy impu-
rities without damaging the yarn.

THE IMPRESARIOS
OF PRATO'S SIDE STREETS

Enjoying a per capita income 50 percent higher than the national average, the workers of Prato, a town northwest of Florence, have every reason to believe that "small is beautiful." With a population of only 160,000 people, Prato boasts 15,000 textile workshops, of which 13,000 have 10 or fewer employees, who are often members of the same family.

The town's reputation as a center of the textile industry was established in the 14th century by Francesco di Marco Datini, who invented the bill of exchange and won lucrative markets in London, Bruges and Florence for the town's weavers of woolen cloth. In the same spirit of free enterprise, Prato's *impresarios* restored the town's prosperity after World War II by recycling rags into clothing for Europe's millions of demobilized soldiers.

Since the 1970s, some of Prato's largest factories have had to close because of foreign competition, but smaller family workshops, weaving every sort of yarn, have continued to prosper. They owe their success partly to low overhead, but mostly to their size, which enables them to react quickly to changes of fashion.

Women scrutinize rolls of material in a Prato factory that specializes in textile finishes — napping, for example, to raise velvety textures. Relatively large and sophisticated outfits such as this are in the minority, and they generally subcontract parts of their work to small family firms.

In a workshop in Prato's suburbs, two brothers operate a loom. Traditionally, small businesses were scattered throughout the town. Today, however, with the increased noise and pollution generated by the machines, the authorities are encouraging firms to move just outside the city.

While his two sons and dog remain absorbed in their own thoughts, a Prato weaver services a machine used in his family business. The casual air of such enterprises belies their profitability: The town's 1980 export earnings from textiles amounted to 1.5 billion dollars.

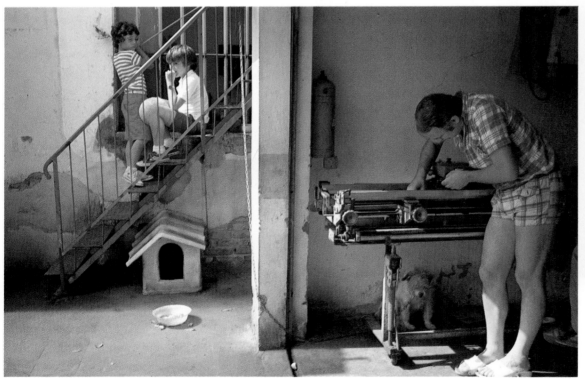

Living and working under the same roof, three generations crowd a workshop while their gun dogs compete for attention. Prato's self-employed cling to rural traditions: They work long hours, but take time off to go hunting or to tend the vegetable gardens that many keep near the town.

Colored threads — destined to become the warp of a patterned fabric — converge on a machine operated by a 70-year-old woman.

A watchful dog keeps its mistress company as she winds white yarn onto a giant spool.

6

In Bologna, where local government has been Communist-run since 1946, a nun attends a party meeting. Pope Pius XII threatened Catholic Communists with excommunication in the 1940s, but today's relationship is one of *ravvicinamento* — or "drawing near" — and stresses common concerns.

THE VOTERS' DILEMMA

To most outsiders, Italy seems to have the most unstable political system in Europe. Governments come and go with extraordinary regularity, and the average duration of postwar administrations has been just 11 months. For weeks at a stretch, Italians survive with a government in virtual suspension, while politicians from four or five parties strive to weld together the next short-lived coalition.

Yet appearances are misleading, because the parties that regularly take a share in government—and the pool from which the senior ministers are drawn—have remained virtually the same for decades. Indeed, one could argue that Italy is politically the most stable country in Europe. The Christian Democrats, a party of the center, emerged after World War II as the strongest group; and in the general election of 1948, the first under Italy's new republican constitution, they were confirmed in power. Since then, they have dominated every one of more than 40 governments, first in alliance with other center and some right-wing parties, later sometimes with the Socialists. The Communists, the other major party, have remained exiled in permanent opposition. Each time the ruling coalition collapses, the crisis is resolved by the creation of a new balance of power that is almost indistinguishable from the old. Nearly always the Christian Democrats control the Interior and Defense ministries, which are responsible for public order and internal and external security.

The constituent assembly that hammered out the new republic's system of government in 1946 and 1947 did not plan on the succession of government collapses that have convulsed the surface of Italian politics. But underlying stability was something that group did strive for. The overriding aim was to keep another dictator like Mussolini from rising to the top, so power was diffused as evenly as possible throughout the system.

Thus Italy has two parliamentary chambers with similar powers, except that only the Chamber of Deputies may initiate legislation. The other chamber, the Senate, has a few appointed members; but the vast majority of its delegates, and the whole of the Chamber of Deputies, are elected by the purest form of proportional representation. A party must win at least 300,000 votes before being admitted to Parliament.

Parliament elects a president for a seven-year term. This head of state has certain prerogatives—including the rights of promulgating laws, calling elections and referendums, dissolving Parliament early (except during the so-called white six months, namely, the last six months of the president's term) and, in consultation with the parties, calling in someone else to put together a new majority government if necessary. The president is also in command of Italy's armed forces.

But in comparison with other democracies, Italy's president is a relatively weak player on the scene; unlike, say, France, with its strong presidency, Italy has nobody who can impose real sanctions and deadlines on bickering parliamentarians. The electoral system also contributes to Italy's succession of short-lived ministries by allowing many small parties a voice in Parliament—with the result that no large party ever commands an overall majority, and coalition government is inescapable. The government's program is a laboriously negotiated compromise between the policies of the various parties; if promises are broken or legislation is delayed, a single party may withdraw from the coalition and wipe out the majority.

But the Italian electoral system also contributes to longer-term stability—amounting almost to paralysis—by ensuring that Parliament faithfully represents the voters' choice. One reason the pattern of parties has remained so constant is that small shifts in allegiance are not distorted into large alterations in parliamentary composition. There have been innumerable occasions since the war when the electorate seemed poised to make a definite break with the tradition of rule by the Christian Democrats and their smaller allies. But always, when the votes were counted, Italians were found to have returned to their traditional loyalties. Such change as did take place was gradual—so gradual, indeed, that the Italians have developed an obsession with decimals. Anyone who was so ignorant as to venture that the Socialists polled 10 percent of the vote in 1983 would be corrected: "No, it was 10.7 percent."

The slow pace of change may be because Italians take their politics very seriously. They affect an outer cynicism toward the political class in general—

6

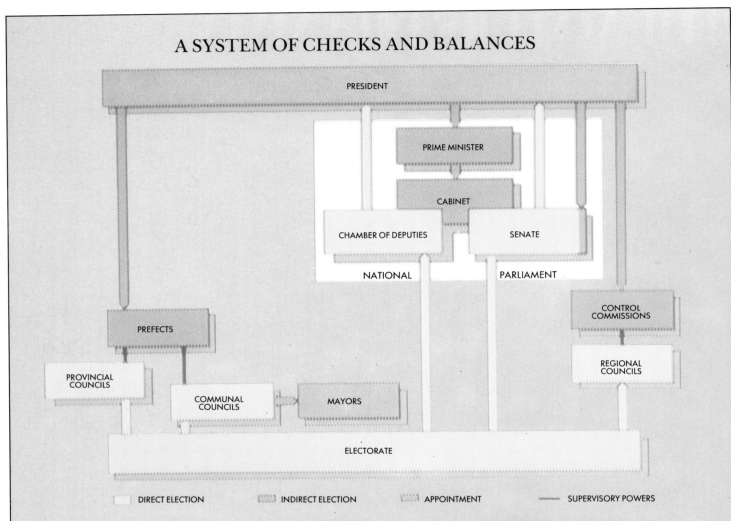

A SYSTEM OF CHECKS AND BALANCES

PRESIDENT

PRIME MINISTER

CABINET

CHAMBER OF DEPUTIES

SENATE

NATIONAL PARLIAMENT

CONTROL COMMISSIONS

PREFECTS

PROVINCIAL COUNCILS

COMMUNAL COUNCILS

MAYORS

REGIONAL COUNCILS

ELECTORATE

DIRECT ELECTION   INDIRECT ELECTION   APPOINTMENT   SUPERVISORY POWERS

Italy is a democratic republic with a parliamentary system of government, designed to restrict the power vested in any individual. The head of state is the president — elected for a seven-year term by Parliament — who is not involved in the day-to-day running of the country. The executive branch consists of the prime minister, appointed by the president, and a cabinet, selected by the prime minister.

Parliament comprises two houses of equal status, which have parallel functions — the Chamber of Deputies, whose members are elected, and the Senate. While almost all of the 315 senators are elected, a handful have been appointed for life by the president.

Besides voting for national representatives, Italians also elect three layers of local deputies. The smallest units of local government are the 8,086 communes, each run by elected councilors and a mayor. Limited local revenues restrict the scope of the councilors,

and at any breakdown in their function, the prefect — a civil servant appointed by the president on the advice of the cabinet — can assume control.

At the next level of local government are 95 provinces, also administered by elected councils. On a still higher level, the elected representatives of the 20 regions have wide legislative powers over areas such as local planning and health services, but their measures must be ratified by a centrally appointed Control Commission.

"they're all crooks" is a common refrain. But the floating, rather flippant vote in the center of the American and British political spectrum is almost unknown in Italy: Voting habits are the product of class, region, religion, family and intellectual evolution in a way that would surprise people in most Western democracies. Turnout is invariably high: At general elections it rarely falls below 80 percent, and in regional and local elections 70 to 80 percent is common. These figures are boosted by the fact that voting is deemed a civic duty in Italy, and failure to vote can be noted on police records; an applicant for a civil-service post who has not voted may have some explaining to do. Nonetheless, the figures are impressive.

The responsible, cautious attitude of voters has been reinforced by the more than usually difficult choice they face. With the Communists as the main opposition party, any abandonment of the status quo would be a leap in the dark that the majority of Italian voters have been unwilling to contemplate. In the early postwar years, a vote for the Communist party appeared to many to mean a vote to join the Soviet bloc. The Italian Communist party has increasingly distanced itself from Moscow, but a residue of fear has remained; whenever the Communists have seemed very likely to increase their share of the poll significantly, the Christian Democrats have been able to cry wolf, scaring wavering constituents back into their time-tested allegiance.

France, like Italy, found itself with a large, well-organized Communist party after the war; the majority of its electorate, like the Italians, rejected the option it represented and instead voted many years for right-of-center governments.

The tiered seats and balconies of the Chamber of Deputies in Rome — one of the two houses of Parliament — provide a theatrical setting for Italy's lawmakers. Above the legislators is a frieze that illustrates the rise of Italian civilization.

6

But in France, the Socialist party was able to reconstruct itself during the late 1960s and overtake the Communists as a major party of the left, making a left-wing government acceptable by 1981. The Italian Socialists have never attained that position, and only since the late 1970s have they become a force to be reckoned with in politics. For most of the postwar period, Italians have been denied any realistic left-wing option other than the Communists.

Perhaps the best place to see the paradoxical steadiness of Italian politics is in a small town. It is there, away from the crowds and banner-waving demonstrators of Rome or Turin or Milan, that Italian democracy finds its bedrock.

Like so many other aspects of small-town life, politics finds its expression, though peaceably enough, out in the streets. It does not dominate: On market days or any other time when people gather, the loudest arguments are likely to be about soccer teams. But somewhere or other there are bound to be a few party political journals pinned up on public display. The Communist *Unità* will certainly be one of them; so, most likely, will be the Socialist *Avanti!* and the Christian Democrat *Il Popolo.* Around each will be a little knot of the *pro* and the *contro,* quietly discussing the issues of the day.

More interesting than the party press are the party posters with which each faction conducts its interminable warfare with the others. These are not the kind of poster that every party's Rome headquarters churns out for national distribution at election time, but the hand-printed — often hand-written — broadsheets by which local squabbles are given a good, ill-tempered airing. The parties always retain their national

character: It can be disconcerting to see the panoply of Marxist jargon deployed in the service of a feud about too many municipal contracts going to the wrong brother-in-law. Only in Italy, perhaps, would a Communist mayor who is also a prosperous businessman denounce his rivals for "antiproletarianism." Such campaigns rarely incite riots, but at least the population knows what is going on.

When national elections come around, the professional politicians take a hand. The arrival of one of them for an election meeting in a small Italian town presents a rare study in contrasts. On the platform, guarded by tough-looking *carabinieri* and backed by even tougher-looking party henchmen, the politician will launch into a set speech. Probably it will be as full of platitudes as such orations usually are in other countries. But it will be delivered with a peculiarly Italian intensity and in high rhetorical style, illustrated with the gestures of a 19th-century tragedian. The audience will listen in a polite silence that is equally studied, interrupting occasionally with applause. Then everyone will quietly leave.

Election day itself is just as low-keyed. It will be a Sunday, the most social day of the Italian week, and it will be more than usually social because many friends and relatives, now living far from home, have taken advantage of the free train tickets provided by the government to encourage them to return to their native commune to vote.

Throughout the day, in a sort of attenuated *passeggiata,* people will amble to and from the polling station. That temple of democracy will be guarded by a teen-age conscript soldier, armed with nothing more ferocious than a scabbarded dress bayonet and — if it is

hot and no superior is nearby — an ice-cream cone. Around the polls there will be much banter between political opponents but rarely bitter abuse. If the party one man supports goes on to win a few more percentage points of the poll, he will not expect the millennium to arrive tomorrow. If one woman's party is knocked back a little, she will not anticipate the end of the world.

Ordinary Italians, loyal though they may be to their party, are all too aware of the gap between politicians' manifestoes and their actions. No matter how sincere the election promises, each party is hobbled by its coalition partners. Only if it can bring other parties around to its way of thinking can it effect change. For this reason, the stuff of Italian politics is power bargaining rather than policy statements, alliances rather than issues.

The Christian Democrats, the party that kept back the left-wing tide for so long, are masters of political survival. They trace their ancestry to the Italian Popular party, founded in 1919 by a priest, Don Luigi Sturzo. Forced underground by Mussolini and the pope, they emerged in the late 1940s as a coalition of anti-Communist forces.

Since then, the party has drawn on four main power bases. The first, the Catholic Church, was especially important in the early postwar years but has declined in significance as the priests' hold on Italians has diminished. In its Catholic schools and universities, the church once trained much of the senior leadership of the party; it also provided a natural hustings — the pulpit.

The second reservoir of support has been the south, together with most of Italy's mountain regions. Old people predominate in these areas — the

In the Sala Clementina, vestibule of the papal apartments, Italian cardinals await an audience with the pope. John Paul II reinstated the regular convening of the College of Cardinals to consult on Church finances, curial reform, and moral and ethical issues.

young having left for the cities of the industrial north — and it is among the old that fear of Communism has been greatest. In the early postwar years, the Christian Democrats undertook extensive land reform in the poorer rural regions, appropriating farms from the big landlords and parceling them out to the peasants. These landowners became ultraconservative and unshakable supporters of the party. But the main reason for its continuing strength is unashamed vote buying; jobs throughout the sprawling bureaucracy are available only to party loyalists. Self-seeking officialdom has been a feature of southern life for centuries; the Christian Democrats have efficiently harnessed the tradition for their own ends.

The third power base of the Christian Democrats has been the middle class, although it has increasingly strayed to vote for smaller parties. Yet even when bourgeois support was at its strongest, Christian Democrats prided themselves in representing the entire class spectrum, rather than just the people who are comfortably placed; indeed, their fourth power base has been a Catholic trade-union wing.

With such diverse support, the Christian Democrats have avoided being pinned too precisely to any one point on the left-right spectrum. They could not be described as a typical Western European Conservative party, since they have not placed special stress on private enterprise and are in favor of a large state-owned industrial sector. They have been fairly responsive to social change in Italy; they have initiated low-cost housing in the major cities, created a health service and enacted laws protecting employees from exploitation. But the Christian Democrats are not altogether a welfare-state party, either, because they believe that members of families must be helped to look after one another, rather than relying on the state to take over; thus, they expect working people to take in their aging parents rather than look to the state to provide homes.

The man who forged the modern Christian Democrat party and who formulated its philosophy was Alcide de Gasperi, a devout Catholic who led a

6

succession of governments from 1946 to 1953. He was an impressive, statesmanlike figure, but his firm leadership eventually ran aground on the political rivalries between different factions of his party. Factionalism has riddled the party ever since. There are always four or five currents with slightly different aims and emphases, which battle continually for dominance. One result is that a new government generally has a different prime minister from the previous one, the fresh face at the top representing a different party clique that has temporarily gained ascendancy.

After the de Gasperi era, the party was dominated by a personal rivalry between two men, Amintore Fanfani and Aldo Moro. Two more opposite figures could hardly be imagined: Fanfani was small, irrepressible, brilliantly articulate, as aggressive as a bull terrier, constantly urging the party in new directions. In the early 1960s, he was the architect of a *rapprochement* with the Socialists. Moro was a tall, gangly, awkward intellectual, given to arcane political maneuvering and interminable, rambling speeches. (He coined the much-mocked phrase "parallel convergences.") His principal goal appeared to be a reconciliation between the Christian Democrats and the Communist party. Moro's delicate negotiations with the Communists were cut short in 1978 when he was assassinated by terrorists. He was replaced as leader of the left wing of his party by Giulio Andreotti, a stooped figure with a sardonic wit and priestly demeanor who became the party's ablest intriguer.

The seesawing fortunes of the factions within the party cannot mask the decline in its popularity. In 1948, it took nearly half the nation's vote; by the 1980s, it was attracting only one

third. One major difficulty is simply its long hold on power, not just in national but also in local and regional government. The party has also lost favor because of its campaigns against divorce and abortion rights; more progressive parties have been on the winning side. Finally, the Christian Democrats have been hit by a succession of scandals.

In the mid-1970s, prominent Christian Democrats were implicated in the Lockheed affair, in which senior officials of the Ministry of Defense were alleged to have taken bribes from executives of the Lockheed company to buy their aircraft. The charges even touched the circle surrounding the nation's president at the time, Giovanni Leone — another Christian Democrat — who was forced to resign in 1978. The scandal of the early 1980s centered on the activities of Freemasons, especially in a lodge code-named P2. There were allegations that the group served as a "state within a state" and had connections with the Mafia and other underworld figures. Lists found by magistrates included not only judges, army officers and members of the security services, but also many prominent Christian Democrats.

The Christian Democrats are also associated with Italy's administrative paralysis. Patronage is so integral to the bureaucracy that far-reaching social reform is impossible under the party's aegis. Any major spending initiative — the Government's Fund for the South, for example, or the reform of the health service, or even emergency relief for earthquake victims — has become a pot of gold to be divided up among local government officials. Such problems should not be exaggerated: They are common to political parties in most countries that have undergone

rapid industrialization, and Italy has made astonishing strides despite them. But the mud clings to the party's name.

The Communists, by contrast, cultivate an image of irreproachable purity. This claim is largely borne out by their record in municipal government; since 1975, they have run most of Italy's big cities in alliance with the Socialists, and on the whole they have kept their hands clean. But of as much interest to the average Italian is their claim to be totally committed to democracy. Over several decades, they have undergone a soul-searching evolution from an orthodox replica of the Soviet mold into something that looks remarkably like a Western-style socialist party.

The germ of the Italian Communist heresy was sown in the 1920s and 1930s by Antonio Gramsci, after an early extremist period under Amadeo Bordiga. Gramsci was an intellectual who spent years in Fascist jails. There he evolved the theory that the Communist party should have a goal beyond "hegemony of the proletariat." Hairsplitting though it may seem at first sight, the implication of this formula was vast: The middle classes would not be totally deprived of a say in government, but they would no longer be allowed to dominate the workers.

Nonetheless, in the early postwar years there was not much to choose between the Italian Communist party and those of Eastern Europe. Stalinists were prominent. Most of its funds came either as grants from the Soviet Union or from a party-controlled import-export agency that arranged deals with the countries of the Eastern bloc. Much of the party's support came from disaffected landless peasants on large estates in what has come to be known as Italy's

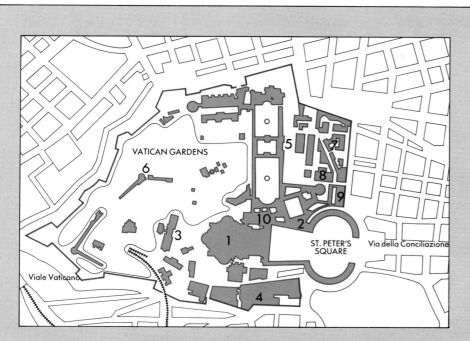

VATICAN GARDENS

ST. PETER'S SQUARE

Via della Conciliazione

Viale Vaticano

A STATE WITHIN A STATE

In the heart of Rome, a yellow and white flag declares the sovereignty of more than 100 walled acres of palaces, gardens, museums and churches. It is the flag of Vatican City, temporal domain of the pope. This territory is home to a shifting population of about 1,000 people and provides a politically independent base for the pope's larger sphere: the Holy See, which has diplomatic ties to nearly 100 countries and governs matters of faith for Roman Catholics the world over.

The Holy See's civil service, the Curia, administers far-flung pastoral and evangelical work, as well as handling the Vatican's complex finances. Although Vatican City is only a remnant of the once-sprawling Papal States, the pope's spiritual jurisdiction continues to grow as the Catholic population approaches 800 million.

1. **St. Peter's Basilica:** the world's largest church, built above the tomb reputed to hold Saint Peter's remains.
2. **The Apostolic Palace:** the papal apartments and leading departments of the Curia.
3. **The Government Palace:** central offices for the administration of the city-state and its art collection.
4. **The Audience Hall:** an auditorium built in 1971 to seat up to 7,000 at weekly audiences with the pope.
5. **The Vatican Library:** a collection of some one million books and documents.
6. **Vatican Radio:** a station broadcasting throughout the world, with religious programs and news in 32 languages.
7. **Offices of *Osservatore Romano*:** the Vatican newspaper, with a circulation of 50,000, publisher of church news and complete texts of papal speeches.
8. **The Polyglot Press:** publisher of missionary texts and papal encyclicals.
9. **The Swiss Guards' Barracks:** home of the Vatican Security Force, 100 Catholic soldiers from Switzerland.
10. **The Sistine Chapel:** meeting place of the College of Cardinals, who elect new popes beneath a ceiling by Michelangelo.

red belt — Tuscany, Emilia-Romagna and Umbria. There were also votes from the masses streaming from the countryside to the cities, with their abysmal social services and housing. Both constituencies wanted dramatic changes in Italian society.

By the early 1970s, the Communists were also winning a following among intellectuals who were disillusioned with Christian Democratic rule. This development placed the party's leadership in a dilemma. To continue winning adherents among the middle classes, the Communists realized they had to distance themselves further from the Soviet model, which was tarnished as a result of the invasions of Hungary in 1956 and Czechoslovakia in 1968. The Italian working class, at that point benefiting from consumer goods for the first time, also began to have its doubts about the virtues of a society in which there would be no private property.

The great leap forward to democratic acceptability came in 1976, after a general election in which the Communist vote shot from 27 to 34 percent. At this time, the head of the Communist Party was Enrico Berlinguer, the small, dour scion of a minor Sardinian aristocratic family. The liberal wing of the party secured an unequivocal statement from Berlinguer that the leadership was committed to democracy — indeed, that it valued democracy above socialism; it accepted the ballot box as the only route to power. The party even began to make its first, timid criticisms of the Soviet model, stressing the need for economic planning and for more social spending, although it had no plans to nationalize more of the economy than was already in public hands. It accepted, in principle, that Italy should

147

Children play in the grounds of their kindergarten, converted from a church. Some 75 percent of Bolognese children attend city nurseries.

Senior citizens enjoy card games in the garden of a municipal community center, a facility that also mounts exhibitions and plays.

SHOWPIECE OF ITALIAN COMMUNISM

Bologna's characteristic arcades line a quiet street.

The university town of Bologna is a procession of arcades, whose red-painted stone porticoes flank nearly every street and square. Behind the medieval colonnades, however, contemporary political dramas are played out, for Bologna is a Communist municipality, the only sizable Italian city to be governed by a predominantly Communist majority continuously since the end of World War II.

With a city council that has often been held up as the most efficient and least corrupt in Italy, Bologna is a showpiece of Communist achievements on a local scale. Its most radical reform has been the decentralization of government. In a system unique for Italy, Bologna is divided into 18 wards, each with its own council mediating between the mayor and the people. The city has tackled urban problems, with successful programs of traffic reform, child care and health care for the elderly.

The most ambitious project has been urban renewal. With their magnificent but dilapidated architectural heritage threatened by developers' bulldozers after the war, the Communists became preservationists. Their plan, still under way, has rescued the historic district by adapting it to modern needs. Old palaces now house libraries and community centers; an old convent is now a preschool.

In the city center, with some 70,000 inhabitants, the municipality is converting privately owned historic property into publicly subsidized housing: The city buys houses and relocates the owners; when the dwellings are repaired and fitted with plumbing, electricity and central heating, the original residents return to the project as renters. Larger buildings, such as churches and palaces, are restored even before civic uses are found for them. Bending the Marxist line, the Bolognese Communists have called on local capitalists to help fund preservation.

remain a member of the North Atlantic Treaty Organization (NATO).

In the years that followed, the party resisted a formal break with the Soviet Union and kept up its habit of bitterly criticizing everything about the United States: its society, its capitalist ethic and especially its foreign policy. The party refused to eject its remaining handful of Stalinists, as critics demanded. But regardless of the Italian Communists' lingering fondness for the Soviet Union, by the time of Berlinguer's sudden death in 1984 they seemed clearly committed to a separate path.

Berlinguer did much to quell fears of Communist power, but he failed to bring his party into government. In 1976, it looked as though there was a chance for the Communists to enter the cabinet. The Socialists, who had been in a series of coalitions with the Christian Democrats, refused to join another government, so the ruling party was compelled to seek support elsewhere. Insisting that the Communists lacked the democratic credentials to join the government, the party's leaders refused to offer them ministerial places but did agree to consult them on major issues in return for support in Parliament and outside. Berlinguer accepted this nebulous arrangement because it seemed a foot in the door of power and a step toward his dream of a "historic compromise" coalition with the Christian Democrats and Socialists. But after the assassination of Aldo Moro in 1978, Berlinguer found, to his surprise, that the Christian Democrats were refusing to move any closer. A year later, in frustration, he withdrew his support, and the government fell.

Failure to achieve the historic compromise forced Berlinguer to look for an alternative strategy. Alliance with

6

the noncommunist left became the Communist party's official policy, although a large part of the Berlinguer wing of the party still hankered after a deal with the Christian Democrats.

The Socialist party could have been the main alternative to the Christian Democrats, were it not for two near-mortal blows that crippled the party in the 1940s and 1960s. The first was an alliance with the Communists in 1948, which chased many moderate politicians out of the party and frightened away many voters. The later blow was the long association with the Christian Democrats from 1963, which led many voters to view the Socialists as the Christian Democrats' plaything.

Shaky strategy was not the least of the Socialists' problems; they also suffered a perpetual identity crisis. In the early postwar years, they regarded the Communists, rather suspiciously, as brothers but differentiated themselves by emphasizing their own allegiance to democracy and the Western alliance. When, in the 1970s, the Communists announced that they, too, were in favor of democracy and NATO, the Socialists were left without distinguishing traits. It was not until the end of the decade that they found a fresh role, thanks to a new leader, Bettino Craxi.

Craxi, a tall, thickset man with a stubborn, puglike expression and a lightning intellect, took over as secretary in 1976. In months, he was imposing his stamp on the party. He replaced its symbol — the hammer and sickle, representing the party's links with the workers — with a carnation. He denounced the Communist party — even in its reformist, post-Berlinguer mode — as "Stalinist." He insisted that the welfare state should be streamlined and espoused environmentalist policies. Then, having reshaped the party, Craxi turned his attention to making the Socialists a force in politics again.

After the 1979 election, when the Christian Democratic-Communist alliance broke up amid mutual recriminations, Craxi made it clear that he would cooperate with the Christian Democrats, but only for a high price: nothing less than the direction of government policy and the post of prime minister. Initially, he had to make do with a compromise candidate — the leader of the small, left-of-center Republican party, Giovanni Spadolini, who in 1981 became the first non-Christian Democratic prime minister since 1945. But by 1983 Craxi was granted the position he had so long coveted.

He acted decisively from the first days of his administration. The government soon raised Italy's international

150

profile and took a tough anti-Soviet line; it was, for example, far more enthusiastic than previous administrations about the placing of NATO anti-Soviet missiles on Italian soil. On the domestic front, Craxi dared to tackle wage indexing, which had been sacrosanct since 1975, and he succeeded in partly cutting the link between inflation and automatic wage increases.

In 1984, he exchanged conciliatory notes with the Communist party, which had been wooing the Socialists since the early 1980s but had received no friendly response. The move brilliantly exploited the Socialists' pivotal position. Despite their meager share of the votes, Craxi had compelled the majority party to depend on him, while for the first time holding out the real possibility of a left-wing alliance that would put the Christian Democrats in opposition.

Italy's colorful smaller parties between them attract some 20 percent of the vote at general elections. These parties perform several vital functions, notably to serve as lightning conductors for those who are disaffected with the Christian Democrats but who do not want to vote for the left, and to act as independent checks on incompetence and corruption in government.

The biggest of the minor parties, the far-right Italian Social Movement, is viewed with some distaste by many others in Italian politics. The party is vigorously nationalist and fiercely anti-Christian Democrat. The inspiration of Mussolini's regime is evident, though the Italian Social Movement denies being a fascist party; if it admitted to the label, it would be banned by Italian law. It draws its support from the lower middle class, from nostalgics with fond memories of Il Duce, and from young people who have a yearning for novelty and adventure.

Some politicians in the party have been accused of connections with terrorism and plots against the state. The leadership has striven to distance itself from these extremists; these efforts have met with only partial success. Opponents continue to charge the party with antidemocratic aspirations, and under no foreseeable circumstances would the Christian Democrats ask it to join a right-of-center coalition.

To the immediate right of the Christian Democrats is the Liberal party, representing the interests of the landowning class and certain segments of the bourgeoisie. The Liberals are persuasive advocates of monetarist economics and of the Western alliance; the Christian Democrats consider them acceptable coalition partners.

The Social Democrats began as an anti-Communist party that broke away from the Socialists in the 1940s, but they have softened their traditional hostility to the Communists a little in recent years. A large part of their support comes from their stalwart defense of Italy's pension system, which acts as a covert government subsidy for millions of Italians for whom it was never intended. (Some five million Italians draw disability pensions, for example, and most of them are able-bodied.) Party members have been implicated in a number of scandals, including the P2 Masonic lodge affair, when the party's leader, Pietro Longo, resigned as budget minister; but the Social Democrats remain a staple of every government coalition.

The Republican party, which began in the 19th century under Giuseppe Mazzini, is the conscience and brain of Italian politics. With only about one Italian in 20 voting for it, its influence far outweighs its size. Under Ugo La Malfa, it established itself as the party calling for sound finance, a functioning welfare state and honesty in public life. La Malfa was succeeded by Giovanni Spadolini, a former editor of Italy's main newspaper, *Corriere della Sera*. His nomination as prime minister in 1981 was a measure of the party's status. Spadolini's government achieved little, but the high moral tone of its public utterances impressed many Italians. Another important Republican is Bruno Visentini, after whom some of the tough mid-1980s tax laws were named.

The Radicals started as a pressure group outside Parliament; in the early 1970s, they campaigned successfully against repealing the new divorce law and in favor of abortion law reform. By 1976, their first delegates were sitting in the Chamber of Deputies. Under the stentorian leadership of Marco Pannella, the party adopted minority causes such as homosexual rights. It also took a strong pro-ecology stand. The Radicals reached their peak of popularity in the late 1970s; in subsequent years, voters grew weary of their constant internal bickering and especially of Pannella's strident appetite for self-publicity, which on one occasion led him to exchange blows with several Communists on the floor of the Chamber of Deputies.

Among the other parties in Parliament are usually one or more from the far left—splinters from the Communist party that advocate revolutionary overthrow of the system. Their numbers are too small to have much impact.

Italy still has minorites on both extremes that oppose the parliamentary system altogether. The far right's strat-

6

egy, such as it is, is to inflame emotions by acts of violence so that gang warfare breaks out; in the ensuing panic, they believe, an authoritarian government would be welcomed. Neofascists were almost certainly responsible for a number of bomb attacks, including an assault on a Milan bank in 1969 and a large explosion at Brescia. The most horrifying incident was a bombing at a Bologna train station in 1980, which took more than 80 lives.

But the number of those involved in right-wing terrorism has never been large, and the threat from the far right was fading by the mid-1980s. The armed forces have never shown the same interest in politics as those of other Latin countries, and without their support the extreme right is unlikely to make much headway politically.

If the far right has shown itself to be sporadically murderous but a political failure, the same cannot be said of the far left, which held Italian democracy at bay for four years from 1976 to 1980. The origins of left-wing terrorism can be traced back to the student and labor unrest of 1968-1969, when a wave of demonstrations ruffled the inertia of Italian politics. Many of the protestors believed that there was no dislodging the Christian Democrats through parliamentary means and that the Communists were too restrained in their tactics. Changes in the university system, which virtually guaranteed anyone a place at college, irrespective of the limited teaching facilities and the even more limited job opportunities for humanities graduates, fueled the frustrations of young people.

There developed a loose extraparliamentary grouping of those who opposed the system altogether. It was called Autonomy, and it may have had

as many as 150,000 adherents at its peak in the early 1970s. Autonomy's leaders were radical university professors, and its intellectual base was in Padua. Within Autonomy, a more organized movement coalesced. From its ranks were drawn the three main terrorist groups of the decade: the Red Brigades, whose recruits came largely from middle-class backgrounds; the working-class Armed Proletarian Nuclei, which operated in Naples and the south; and Front Line, an organization that was looser and more disparate than the other two. Myriad smaller groups also sprang up.

The founders of the Red Brigades were a married couple, Margherita (Mara) Cagol and Renato Curcio, who had been sociology students together at the University of Trento. Comfortably well-off, apparently destined for careers in chemistry and accounting respectively, they instead drifted underground and began to see themselves as the elite leadership that would bring about the revolution on behalf of the masses. By the early 1970s, they had built up a clandestine military organization around them. Its objective was to set up an "armed party" that would overthrow the "diseased organs" of the Italian state, or would provoke such a counterreaction from the authorities that the proletarians would flock to join party ranks. There was much speculation about possible international connections between the Red Brigades and Czechoslovakia, the Palestinians or Libya, among others, but none received definite confirmation.

In the early days, the Red Brigades' crimes consisted mainly of damage to property — burning the cars of factory bosses, for example — but, becoming bolder and more vicious, they gradu-

ated to armed robbery and murder. From shooting policemen, the Brigades progressed to shooting journalists, magistrates (in an effort to keep members from being tried), industrialists and, eventually, politicians.

By 1978, Mara Cagol was dead, mowed down in a shoot-out with the police, and Renato Curcio had been tracked down and imprisoned. He and a number of other founders were awaiting a trial, which was repeatedly put off for fear of reprisals. Only momentarily nonplussed by the disappearance of their leaders, the Red Brigades had rallied themselves and quickly evolved into a more deadly and efficient organization than before.

Their forces were now elaborately divided into almost-autonomous cells, ensuring nearly perfect security for the upper ranks and for each independent branch, no matter how many of the humble operatives were captured. All ranks, however, submitted themselves to the rigid, almost monastic rules prescribed for daily life. Hair was to be cut short, beards were forbidden, meals were to be eaten at home, bedtime was before midnight, apartments were to be kept clean and tidy, guns were to be carried at all times.

With this discipline, the Red Brigades were capable of carrying out more elaborate crimes than ever before. Meticulously, they developed plans to stage a master coup. Their goal was nothing less than to capture Italy's leading politician.

On the morning of March 16, ex-prime minister Aldo Moro was being driven to Parliament from the small church he attended daily. Followed by an escort vehicle, his car moved slowly down Rome's Via Fani. A car suddenly backed into the street, blocking the way forward. Moro's chauffeur jammed on the brakes, and the escort crashed into the back of the car.

The ambushers jumped from their car and sprayed the scene with bullets. Moro was seized and manhandled into a waiting vehicle. The kidnappers then sped off, leaving the corpses of the bodyguards lying in the street.

Moro was held for nearly two months by his Red Brigade captors. While the police searched fruitlessly, pictures of him in his captivity were circulated, together with letters that he was somehow induced or forced to write, pleading for negotiations to be opened and hinting at dark revelations he might be obliged to make. Then on May 9, acting on a tip, police discovered his body in the trunk of a Renault, parked as a symbolic gesture halfway between the Christian Democratic and Communist headquarters in central Rome. It was a supreme gesture of contempt for authority by the terrorists.

But the cold-blooded murder won no sympathy among the public; and the state reacted to it, with commendable

restraint, by introducing laws of preventive detention (later withdrawn) that only marginally tightened existing legislation. The tide began to turn against the terrorists.

At this crucial point, a new interior minister, Virginio Rognoni, was appointed to oversee Italy's three main police forces — the *carabiniere,* or paramilitary police; the treasury police, whose original role of tracking down tax evaders has expanded in many directions; and the regular police. Carlo Alberto Dalla Chiesa, a *carabiniere* general, was appointed head of an elite antiterrorist detachment. To break the shield of secrecy with which the Brigades protected themselves, a law was passed allowing terrorists who informed on their comrades to receive considerably reduced prison sentences.

Aided by this measure, Dalla Chiesa scored spectacular successes in cracking Red Brigades cells. His technique was to insert one man into a cell, or column, which was in contact with another cell only through a single member. The infiltrator would identify who the key member was; the police would then arrest and interrogate that person, using

the prospect of the reduced jail sentence as an inducement to talk. The Milan column of the Red Brigades was the first to be thoroughly broken; the Genoa, Turin and Rome columns followed shortly afterward. Some 400 arrests of suspected terrorists were made in less than three years. By 1982, terrorism had been all but defeated in Italy; the Red Brigades themselves acknowledged that their dream of a civil war in Italy was lost.

Dalla Chiesa's success in dealing with the Red Brigades was so spectacular that the government of the day decided to employ him in tackling more deep-rooted problems; the Mafia, its Calabrian cousin the 'Ndrangheta and the Neapolitan Camorra. But the outcome was very different. Just four months after Dalla Chiesa was sent to Palermo, he was shot dead by Mafia gunmen.

This catastrophe did not deter the Italian government from continuing the battle against the Mafia. In the mid-1980s, notable progress was made in rounding up Mafia criminals, once again by encouraging key figures to talk. But even the most optimistic of Italians are resigned to a long, hard

Slogans are outnumbered by declarations of love on the "prow" of the Isola Tiberina, a hospital island in the Tiber River near Trastevere. Graffiti have a long history: The walls of Pompeii carry political and amorous scribblings made in the first century A.D.

6

struggle against the Mafia and the other secret organizations before they can be overcome.

The Italian state's successful fight against terrorism showed it at its decisive best. But in less grave situations, firm leadership is all too rare; the system militates against it. Because of faction fighting within the parties and the danger of the strongest party alienating any one of its coalition partners, all change must be reached by consensus, a slow and painful business. One result is that governments invariably have great difficulty in enforcing their authority over other institutions — trade unions, employers and the bureaucracy, for example. The shortcomings of the system are also visible in the international field. The merry-go-round of Italian prime ministers has made it difficult for any one of them to acquire an international reputation. As a result, Italy has been less effective than the other major partners within NATO or the EEC in terms of making its voice heard, although its commitment to both is passionate.

Italians are well aware of the lack of decisive leadership, and proposals to remedy it abound. The Socialists, in particular, have pressed for constitutional reform. One possibility would be to strengthen the president's powers — but this is unlikely to find favor, as Italians recoil from any weakening of Parliament. Another possibility is to strengthen the power of the prime minister vis-à-vis his own party and those in coalition with him. At present the premier, though allowed to choose the cabinet, is in practice obliged to listen to the party secretaries — whose chief concern is that each faction gets its due share of seats. Change in the electoral system has also been proposed, to allow only parties with 5 percent or more of the vote to sit in Parliament; such a rule would force the small parties to merge into bigger groups and might lead to more stable coalitions. But the very inertia of the political system makes radical constitutional reform unlikely in the near future.

Italians are fond of saying that they are governed best when they are not governed at all. That is untrue: Italy could be governed much more effectively than it is. However, the system is considerably more resilient than most outsiders realize, and Italians are more content with it than their grumbles might suggest. The recurring government crises are so predictable that they do not unduly hold up the administrative processes and, despite the obstacles, surprisingly far-reaching reforms have been enacted.

Most fundamental and impressive is the fact that Italy has come through its postwar industrial revolution without succumbing to authoritarian rule. Few countries have experienced the development of an urban, manufacturing economy without suffering serious upheaval or repression. In Italy's Mediterranean neighbors, Greece and Turkey, political disturbances were followed by a bout of autocratic government; Spain and Portugal were ruled by dictators throughout the process of industrialization. Yet Italy managed to contain the social unrest that was engendered by its great drive toward national prosperity. For its stability, Italy must spare some gratitude for the constitution, which guards against extremist tendencies. But most of all it must thank its level-headed voters, staunchly committed to their ramshackle, but functioning, democracy. □

With swords frozen in salute, a detachment of the ceremonial guards known as the Corazzieri lines a corridor in the Quirinal Palace, the official presidential residence. Recruits for the unit — honor escort to the president and visiting heads of state — must be at least 6 feet 2 inches tall.

ACKNOWLEDGMENTS

The index for this book was prepared by Vicki Robinson. The editors also thank: Sam Allis, Rome; Federica Bellici, Paolo Ricci, Italian Tourist Office, London; Mike Brown, London; Marco Cagnoni, Pietrasanta; Caposio e Lauria, Architects' Studio, Turin; Catholic Media Society, London; Windsor Chorlton, London; Conte Piero Milano d'Aragona, Turin; Conte Xavier de Maistre, Turin; Fiat Press Office, Turin; Caroline Hill, London; Martin Leighton, Hove; Jacqueline Long, The Lighting Workshop, London; Catherine Mcnabb, London; Simon Mitchell, Marcatré Limited, London; *La Nazione*, Prato; Enrico Nori, Carrara; Diego Novelli, Turin; Robin Olson, London; Vittorio Prayer, Town Council, Carrara; Enzo Ragazzini, Rome; Malise Ruthven, London; Renzo Salvadori, Venice; Roger Stewart, Sutton; Ruth Sullivan, London; Deborah Thompson, London; Unione Industriale, Prato; the staff of the Library of the Italian Institute, London.

PICTURE CREDITS

BIBLIOGRAPHY

BOOKS

Acton, Harold, *The Last Bourbons of Naples.* London: Methuen, 1961.

Allum, P. A.:
Italy: Republic without Government? London: Weidenfeld and Nicolson, 1973.
Politics and Society in Postwar Naples. Cambridge: Cambridge University Press, 1973.

Ardagh, John, *A Tale of Five Cities.* London: Secker and Warburg, 1979.

Arlacchi, Pino, *Mafia, Peasants and the Great Estates.* Cambridge: Cambridge University Press, 1983.

Barzini, Luigi:
From Caesar to the Mafia. London: Hamish Hamilton, 1971.
The Italians. Middlesex, England: Penguin Books, 1968.

Bethemont, Jacques, and Jean Pelletier, *Italy: A Geographical Introduction.* London: Longman, 1983.

Blue Guides:
Blanchard, Paul, *Southern Italy.* London: Benn, 1982.
Macadam, Alta, ed., *Northern Italy.* London: Benn, 1978.
Macadam, Alta, ed., *Sicily.* London: Benn, 1975.
Rossiter, Stuart, *Rome.* London: Benn, 1975.

Bull, George, *Inside the Vatican.* London: Hutchinson, 1982.

Caesar, Michael, and Peter Hainsworth, eds., *Writers and Society in Contemporary Italy.* Leamington Spa, England: Berg, 1984.

Cairns, Christopher, *Italian Literature: The Dominant Themes.* Newton Abbot: David and Charles, 1977.

Cantacuzino, Sherban, and Susan Brandt, *Saving Old Buildings.* London: Architectural Press, 1980.

Castronno, Valerio, *L'Industria Italiana dall' Ottocento a Oggi.* Milan: Mondadori, 1980.

Chamberlain, Samuel, *Italian Bouquet.* London: Hamish Hamilton, 1958.

Chamberlin, E. R., and the Editors of Time-Life Books, *Rome* (The Great Cities series). Amsterdam: Time-Life Books, 1976.

Chandler, S. B., and J. A. Molinara, *The Culture of Italy.* Toronto: Griffon House, 1979.

Clark, Kenneth:
Landscape into Art. London: Murray, 1979.
Leonardo da Vinci. Middlesex, England: Penguin Books, 1958.

Clough, Shepard B., *The Economic History of Modern Italy.* New York: Columbia University Press, 1964.

Cornelisen, Ann, *Women of the Shadows.* London: Macmillan, 1976.

Davis, John H., and the Editors of Newsweek Book Division, *Venice.* New York: Newsweek, 1973.

Deaglio, Mario, and Giuseppe de Rita, *Il Punto sull'Italia.* Milan: Mondadori, 1983.

de Mauro, Tullio, *Storia Linguistica dell'Italia Unita.* Bari: Editori Laterza, 1963.

Fodor's Guide to Italy. London: Hodder and Stoughton, 1983.

Gardiner, Stephen, *The Evolution of the House.* London: Constable, 1975.

Gendel, Milton, ed., *An Illustrated History of Italy.* London: Weidenfeld and Nicolson, 1966.

Grant, Michael, *The World of Rome.* London: Sphere Books, 1960.

Guide to Italy. Florence: Bonechi, 1984.

Gunn, Peter, *A Concise History of Italy.* London: Thames and Hudson, 1971.

Hadas, Moses, and the Editors of Time-Life Books, *Imperial Rome* (The Great Ages of Man series). New York: Time-Life Books, 1965.

Hale, J. R., ed., *A Concise Encyclopedia of the Italian Renaissance.* London: Thames & Hudson, 1981.

Hamilton, Olive, *The Divine Country.* London: André Deutsch, 1982.

Hearder, H., and D. P. Waley, *A Short History of Italy.* Cambridge: Cambridge University Press, 1980.

Hobsbawm, E. J., *Primitive Rebels.* Manchester, England: Manchester University Press, 1972.

Johnson, Hugh, *Wine Companion.* London: Mitchell Beazley, 1983.

Jucker, Ninetta, *Italy.* London: Thames and Hudson, 1970.

Katz, Robert, *Days of Wrath: The Public Agony of Aldo Moro.* London: Granada, 1980.

Kelly, Francis, *Art Restoration.* Newton Abbot: David and Charles, 1971.

Kubly, Herbert, *Italy.* London: Sunday Times, 1961.

Levi, Carlo, *Christ Stopped at Eboli.* Transl. by Frances Frenaye. Middlesex, England: Penguin Books, 1982.

Lowe, Alfonso, *La Serenissima.* London: Cassell, 1974.

Lutz, Vera, *Italy: A Study in Economic Development.* Westport, Conn.: Greenwood Press, 1975.

Mack Smith, Denis:
Garibaldi. London: Hutchinson, 1957.
Italy. Ann Arbor: University of Michigan, 1969.
Mussolini. London: Weidenfeld and Nicolson, 1981.

Malaparte, Curzio, *Maledetti Toscani.* Florence: Vallecchi, 1976.

Marinetti, Filippo, *Selected Writings.* Transl. by R. N. Flint and A. A. Coppotelli. London: Secker and Warburg, 1972.

Martinelli, Roberto, and Antonio Padellaro, *Il Delitto Moro.* Milan: Rizzoli, 1979.

Masson, Georgina, *The Companion Guide to Rome.* London: Fontana, 1974.

Menen, Aubrey, and the Editors of Time-Life Books, *Venice* (The Great Cities series). Amsterdam: Time-Life Books, 1976.

Michelin Tourist Guide, *Italy.* Paris: Michelin, 1983.

Morris, James, *Venice.* London: Faber and Faber, 1960.

Morton, H. V., *A Traveller in Rome.* London: Methuen, 1966.

Nichols, Peter, *Italia, Italia.* London: Macmillan, 1973.

Norwich, John Julius, ed., *The Italian World.* London: Thames and Hudson, 1983.

Procacci, Giuliano, *History of the Italian People.* London: Weidenfeld and Nicolson, 1970.

Pucci, Eugenio, *The Vatican City.* Florence: Bonechi, 1972.

Pulgram, Ernst, *The Tongues of Italy.* Cambridge, Mass.: Harvard University Press, 1958.

Ridley, Jasper, *Garibaldi.* London: Constable, 1974.

Romano, Sergio, *Italie.* Paris: Editions du Seuil, 1979.

Sand, Maurice, *Masques et Bouffons.* Paris: Michel and Lezy Frères, 1860.

Scalfari, Eugenio, and Giuseppe Turani, *Razza Padrona: Storia della Borghesia de Stato.* Milan: Feltrinelli, 1975.

Shipman, David, *The Great Movie Stars: The International Years.* London: Angus and Robertson, 1980.

Silone, Ignazio, *Fontamara.* Milan: Mondadori, 1967.

Starr, Chester G., *The Ancient Romans.* New York: Oxford University Press, 1971.

Stendhal:
The Private Diaries. Transl. by Robert Sage. London: Victor Gollancz, 1955.
Rome, Naples and Florence. Transl. by Richard N. Coe. London: John Calder, 1959.
Vie de Rossini. Ed. by Henri Martineau. Paris: Le Divan Press, 1929.

Tisdall, Caroline, and Angelo Bozzono, *Futurism.* London: Thames and Hudson, 1977.

Trease, Geoffrey, *The Italian Story.* London: Macmillan, 1963.

von Heintze, Helga, *Roman Art.* London: Weidenfeld and Nicolson, 1972.

Willey, David, *Italians.* London: BBC Publications, 1984.

Wiskemann, Elizabeth, *Italy since 1945.* London: Macmillan, 1971.

PERIODICALS

Arlacchi, Pino, "L'Etica Mafiosa e lo Spirito del Capitalismo." *Le Scienze,* June 1984.

"Bologna Commune." *Modulo,* October/November 1978.

Economist:
"Eppur si Muove: A Survey of Italy." July 23, 1983.
"Italian Economy Survey." May 23, 1981.
"Nirvana by Numbers." December 24, 1983.

Ellis, William S., "Surviving Italian Style." *National Geographic,* February 1984.

Financial Times (London):
"Italian Engineering." July 16, 1984.
"Survey: Italy." December 20, 1983.

Fox, Robert:
"Beyond Eboli." *Listener,* April 21, 1983.
"An Italian Romance." *Listener,* April 14, 1983.
"Marsala, Missiles and Mafia." *Listener,* April 28, 1983.

Gore, Rick:
"The Mediterranean." *National Geographic,* December 1982.
"A Prayer for Pozzuoli." *National Geographic,* May 1984.

Hall, Stephen S., "Puppets and Passion." *Geo,* April 1984.

Hamblin, Dora Jane, "The Luthier's Art." *Smithsonian,* October 1983.

Newman, Cathy, "Carrara Marble." *National Geographic,* July 1982.

Panorama:
"Droga: Guerra ai Merchanti Della Morte." April 23, 1984.
"Quanto Pesa l'Elefante." March 5, 1984.

Time:
"The Entrepreneurs of Prato." August 17, 1981.
"Furor over Fiddles in Cremona." April 10, 1984.

The Times (London):
"Italian Regions." June 16, 1983.
"Special Report: Italy." November 4, 1983.
"Special Report: Italy." October 31, 1984.

Warner, Marina, "The Palio." *Connoisseur,* June 1984.

INDEX

Page numbers in italics refer to illustrations or illustrated text.

Time-Life Books Inc. offers a wide range of fine
recordings, including a *Big Bands* series. For
subscription information, call 1-800-621-7026,
or write TIME-LIFE MUSIC, Time & Life
Building, Chicago, Illinois 60611.